Marriage in the Whirlwind is a warm, touching, funny, yet practical book with specific help for stressed-out couples. Bill and Pam write from real life: they have been there—are there—living in the whirlwind. We personally know that they are managing the stress of their whirlwind yet are deeply connected to each other, to their three boys and to God.

JIM AND SALLY CONWAY
Codirectors, Mid-Life Dimensions
Authors, Traits of a Lasting Marriage

Bill and Pam unmistakably touch the relentless challenge of marital relationships in these frantic times. Their analyses are uncannily accurate and penetrating, their prescriptions fresh and eminently usable.

DENNIS DIRKS
Dean, Talbot School of Theology

Within the last few years, life's pace seems to have taken a quantum leap. It feels like just yesterday the concept of "overnight" seemed amazingly fast. Yet today when we really need something we fax or e-mail it and it is there in seconds! In this kind of world, where needs are "now" and "immediate," the relationship advice and approaches of even a decade ago seem unrealistic and antiquated.
Taking into consideration all the pressures and stresses of life today, Bill and Pam Farrel have created a practical and workable guide for keeping intimacy in marriage alive and well.

FLORENCE LITTAUER
President, CLASS Speakers, Inc.
Author, After Every Wedding Comes a Marriage

Who wouldn't want to trade nonstop activity for intimacy? Hurried minutes together for long moments of closeness? But *how?* In *Marriage in the Whirlwind,* the Farrels give couples tangible, biblical advice on exchanging the fast track for more fun and fulfillment. From granting forgiveness to actually *gaining* closeness through technology, I found their book wonderfully readable and filled with take-home applications.

JOHN TRENT
President, Encouraging Words
Author, I'd Choose You

This was a helpful book for me, since I am caught up in the whirlwind of a global ministry. I highly recommend it.

NEIL T. ANDERSON
President, Freedom in Christ Ministries

MARRIAGE
in the
WHIRLWIND

7 Skills for Couples Who Can't Slow Down

BILL & PAM FARREL

InterVarsity Press
Downers Grove, Illinois

InterVarsity Press® is the book-publishing division of InterVarsity Christian Fellowship®, a student movement active on campus at hundreds of universities, colleges and schools of nursing in the United States of America, and a member movement of the International Fellowship of Evangelical Students. For information about local and regional activities, write Public Relations Dept., InterVarsity Christian Fellowship, 6400 Schroeder Rd., P.O. Box 7895, Madison, WI 53707-7895.

ISBN 0-8308-1953-3

Printed in the United States of America ∞

Library of Congress Cataloging-in-Publication Data

Farrel, Bill, 1959-
    Marriage in the whirlwind: hope for couples who can't slow down/
Bill and Pam Farrel.
        p.   cm.
    Includes bibliographical references.
    ISBN 0-8308-1953-3 (pbk.: alk. paper)
    1. Married people—Religious life.   2. Marriage—Religious
aspects—Christianity.   I. Farrel, Pam, 1959- .   II. Title.
BV4596.M3F37   1996
248.8'44—dc20   *96-17398*
                                                            CIP

18	17	16	15	14	13	12	11	10	9	8	7	6	5	4	3	2	1
11	10	09	08	07	06	05	04	03	02	01	00	99	98	97	96		

To our best friends in the whirlwind
(you just happen to be our family too!)
Bret and Erin
Deney and Phil
Jim and Kathy
Lori and Lee

His way is in the whirlwind and the storm,
and the clouds are the dust of his feet. . . .
The LORD is good, a refuge in times of trouble.
He cares for those who trust in him.
Nahum 1:3, 7

1

HOW DID
WE GET IN THIS
WHIRLWIND?

*Y*ou hear the sound of an oncoming locomotive. The sky seems blacker than night. The pressure in the air makes you feel as if your head will explode any minute. Impending danger is near. You can smell its putrid destruction in the air. The wind whips in and begins to carry off everything you've worked so hard to acquire.

You run to get your family. You all dive under the bed for cover, hoping it will keep you safe. Everyone is shaking.

In the pitch darkness you hear the roof give way. A biting cold torrent enters the room. You look up. The open sky swirls ominously above you. For a moment, you feel as if everything and everyone you love is being taken away from you. Panic races like frigid blood through your veins. You peek out, and your worst fears are confirmed. You are in the eye of the storm.

A whirlwind has landed on you! And you wonder what to do now—whether you should stay put and pray or try to get out from under this horrendous monster and run for your life.

That's how survivors of tornadoes sound when they describe their experience. But it may also be an accurate description of how you and your spouse feel in this hectic, fast-paced, technologically inundated yet virtually unpredictable world in which we all live. How did we get in this whirlwind anyway?

Hurricane Alert

The newspapers carried a bold headline: "Bigger, Stronger, Closer: South Florida Bracing for Hurricane Andrew." On the radio, the civil defense coordinator barked out advice: "Above all, do not panic . . ."[1]

Don't panic; prepare. The first step in preparation, though, is to realize that the hurricane is coming. Strong winds prevail; a storm is on its way. Too many of us are feeling the barometric pressure dropping in our lives, but we refuse to call the situation a storm.

After our move to San Diego, the housing market soared. We were priced right out of the market. There were absolutely no homes, not even disheveled fixer-uppers, that we could afford. We thought about renting, but the difference between paying rent and paying on a mortgage at the time was minimal. We'd been pastoring the church for nearly a year, and we really felt God wanted us to be rooted for the long run. At the time, it was a seller's market. People would offer more than the seller's asking price, trying to outbid each other. There was simply not enough available housing at the time—especially entry-level homes.

Our church was composed of many tradespeople in construction. One after another, they began to offer their services, for free, to help us build our own home.

We resisted at first. We knew it would be a challenge to build a home and build the church at the same time. We prayed. We listed the pros and cons. We decided we really didn't want to build a home. We searched the market again and came to the same agonizing conclusion—if we wanted a home we were going to have to build it ourselves! Finally, through a series of remarkable events, some key needs were met. We bought property, designed plans and began to build. (For several years, Bill had studied architecture, then had been a draftsman, so he designed our house to try to fit into our budget.) We interviewed people who'd built their own homes. We interviewed contractors. We estimated the cost and the time. We then doubled our estimates just to make sure we'd have enough resources.

To make a long story short, even our expanded estimates were wrong! It took twice as much time and more money than expected to complete the house. An article even appeared in the local paper because everyone knew we were trying to beat the stork. Pam was expecting, and we wanted to finish the house before the baby came.

Pam's mom called and volunteered to come two weeks before the baby and help move us in. When she arrived, she and Pam began packing and moving things into the garage of the home because last-minute items (like flooring) needed to be finished before the building inspector would let us move in.

When loading the trunk of our car, Mom noticed that there was no spare tire. She asked Pam about it, and Pam gave her standard answer that she'd given everyone during the past several months. "Bill wants to get to it. He just hasn't had time. He's working full-time at church and full-time at the house. I'm more worried that he's not getting enough sleep. If I get a flat, I'll just call Bill or someone. God will take care of me."

To that Pam's mom responded, "Isn't that asking God to do your work?"

"Well, I've been driving around all these months without a spare and I haven't got a flat. God and I have this deal!"

Pam and her mom started laughing as Mom said, "I don't think God makes deals like that."

"You're right. I don't think God makes deals either—but he has taken care of me."

Mom unloaded the trunk, then went in to find Bill. Pam was carrying boxes behind her.

"Bill, you know I am not one of those bossy mothers-in-law."

"No, Mom. You're great." Bill said.

"I'd never interfere with your and Pam's life. I'm really proud of you."

"Thanks, Mom," Bill said cautiously.

"But Bill, you've been letting your pregnant wife drive around on errands all over this county for you, and there's no spare tire in her car! What if she got a flat? *You can't live this way!*"

"I know we can't live this way!" Bill agreed with a sigh.

"No, we can't live this way!" Pam echoed. We all laughed, and Mom gave us both a hug. But we all knew we *couldn't* go on living this way. We were in a whirlwind, and we had to get out. We had to survive this one and regroup before another storm could form.

Because we know what a whirlwind feels like, we can read the telltale signs on the weary faces around us in this world. Many times it seems couples long to cry out, "Stop the world—I want to get off!" Whirlwinds come in all shapes and sizes, but there are skills that can help you two corral the wind and give you a successful marriage no matter what storm brews on the horizon. Those skills are the topic of this book.

The Uncontrollable Wind

Just like natural disasters, sometimes a whirlwind lands on your life for no apparent reason. It could have been a job loss, an economic downturn in the market, the shrinking of your paycheck. Maybe it was an injury or illness that hit your happy home and tore the roof off your heart. Perhaps it was a move, even a promotion. Maybe you are doing everything right but the ever-increasing pace of modern life and the constant demand to adapt to new technology has you running to keep up. Circumstances beyond our control can place us in the eye of the storm.

Lee and Maggie were happy, even blissful at times. Everything was so good. They had a nice house and some great friendships; Lee was doing a terrific job at work; Maggie was enjoying being a mom and a freelance artist. The kids were happy and healthy—until the blood work came back on little James. It was leukemia.

Tests. Treatments. Mounting bills—even with insurance. Life was becoming a blur accompanied by an aching heart. The tornado had touched down.

The Techno-Wind

Technology can whip into our lives and rattle the windows. Life is supposed to be easier now with fax machines, answering machines, voice mail, e-mail, personal computers, modems, Internet, pagers, portable phones—on and on it comes down the information highway. If all this technology is supposed to create more time, then why are we all so busy? Is there a way to use technology to get out of the whirlwind instead of being carried away by it?

Marianne and Cameron kept trying to hold their marriage together. Life was just moving so fast. First, they tried pagers so they could keep track of one another. Then they tried cellular phones so they could talk on demand. Then they invested in e-mail and an 800 number, but it was becoming more and more difficult to feel close to one another. They were married, but, because of two very demanding careers, they were hardly ever in the same city, let alone the same house.

"I don't know what else to try," said Cameron.

"We could try being together," said Marianne.

"Who's going to give up what to do that?"

Differing expectations bring conflict, but no one wants to throw theirs out. We want our own rights and agendas. Flying debris makes the air feel heavy and the sky look dark.

The Emotional Wind

Some storms sneak up on you. They run so close to the ground that they may seem to be just a short summer rain. Often internal storms are this way. You may have been cruising through life with your heart's convertible top down; then—boom!—suddenly rain and hail are pelting you and raining on your personal parade. Past decisions, mislaid priorities, poor lifestyle choices or unresolved baggage from your past can create an emotional electrical storm in your life. One day life was great. The next day the power is out, the heat's off, and you feel all alone as you stare out the window of your life and watch the raindrops silently drip down the windowpanes of your heart.

Some storms seem like they'll never end. The Monroes thought their problems were behind them. Their early years had been full of turmoil personally and financially. They had gained it all; then they lost it all! They had hoped a move to a new location, a fresh start would change it all—but it didn't. Jobs never lasted. Now, their careers continued to spiral downward. Decisions from their past haunted their future. Their commitment to each other had never been stronger, but they felt they'd never worked so hard to stay in love.

They felt like they wanted to huddle together in the closet and just wait the hurricane out.

"Get Out of My Way, Wind—I Have to Provide!"

In the past several years the cost of living has increased greatly. But spendable income has not. Couples today can kiss the American dream goodby! Gone are the days when one income will provide for two cars, a home in the suburbs, a family cabin on the lake, college tuition, orthodontic work and piano lessons. For many families, of course, those days never really existed. And today, just putting bread on the table and a roof over the family's head is hard-earned success!

It's a good thing *Ozzie and Harriet* is no longer on the air. Today, Ozzie would probably leave Harriet for a younger woman, and Harriet would then marry a man with child-support payments and huge credit-card bills! Providing for a family has become a fight for survival. Men and women mount up like gallant knights of the round table and try to slay the beastly dragon of high inflation, escalating housing costs and corporate downsizing.

More and more time seems to be spent working. A time survey commissioned by the Hilton hotel chain discovered that the average American home has seven clocks; nearly half the population feels lost without a watch; and Americans estimate they have only nineteen hours of free time a week, which is at least seven less than they desire.[2] Time seems to keep slipping right through our fingers.

"We work hard and we still don't make it. I keep hoping it's just because we're spending too much, but we keep cutting the budget and we still can't make it. The stress on our marriage is getting worse. We love each other, but that doesn't seem to be enough," said Jim with a worried frown.

His wife, Teresa, nodded. "I'm scared."

In Greek mythology, Daedalus, an artist and inventor of the labyrinth, and his son Icarus were imprisoned on Crete. Daedalus created wings so the two could fly off their island prison. Icarus loved the wings his father had made for him. His father gave only one warning: "Don't fly too near the sun. The wax that fastens your wings will melt from the heat." But Icarus loved the feeling of soaring, flying higher and higher, higher than anyone had ever gone. He was so carried away in the thrill of soaring that he failed to notice how near to the sun he had gotten. The wings melted off and he plunged to his death.

Personal achievement can make us like Icarus. Sometimes our desire to soar higher and higher puts us too near the heat of the sun. We want just a little bit more, a little bit sooner. Then our wings melt and we find ourselves in the center of a death spiral! We chase the dream too long with our eyes focused on what could be if we only worked a little harder.

"Time Is Too Short!"

For many, the cause is noble. Save the whales, save the environment, save the hungry, save the world. Some couples pursue their mission so intensely that they lose sight of their marriage. They rightly sense the time is short and the need great, but while fighting for the cause they find themselves fighting each other. Caregivers are especially vulnerable. They are so busy caring for others that they forget to care for themselves.

"It just happened so gradually. We didn't realize how far apart we'd drifted. We marched together, rallied the troops, put on press conferences. Our calendar was full with important appointments except the most important of all—time for each other." Gary reached across the sofa and picked up Rena's hand.

"We almost won the world, and lost each other—almost."

The Secret Storm of Success

"Of the two struggles, I am convinced that prosperity is a much greater test than adversity. Prosperity is far more deceptive," notes bestselling author Charles Swindoll.[3] Sometimes prosperity brings its own storm. Sudden success can create an emotional whirlwind. Suddenly, everyone is a "friend." You can afford anything and everything, so you buy it. New social relationships form while old relationships fizzle. Free time may disappear as you struggle to hold on to the business tiger you created!

Success can be thrilling. You're in the limelight and loving it—that is, until you find that your name in lights equals no privacy. Having it all means managing it all—all the time. Or your swelling head becomes too much for your spouse to take.

Tabloids are full of couples who land the big recording contract and sign the big movie deals. Their romantic adventure is detailed in the press. But before the printing press can cool, the news of their marriage on the rocks is reported.

Why All the Alarm?

In Pass Christian, a small Mississippi tourist town, Police Chief Jerry Peralta drove up and down the highway, stopping at every door. "Evacuate!" he cried. A hurricane was headed their way. Some listened. Others laughed. At one apartment complex, a large group gathered with kegs of beer for a hurricane party. They'd been through a few hurricanes before, and they thought they were kind of fun.

The storm hit at ten that night. A wave three stories high crashed in on the apartment building. The building was torn apart, and the dead bodies were spread across Pass Christian. The next day, one little five-year-old boy was found floating on a mattress—the only survivor of the party.

You may be thinking, "My life is just fine. Sure, I sometimes long for more quiet days. I love the front porch swing, reading in a hammock, long talks by a roaring fire. But I can handle things." But if you think the whirlwind will never touch down on your life, you are wrong. The whirlwind knows no boundaries. The best preparation for the wind is to know the signs and know the skills it will take to navigate through the storm.

Don't Chase Twisters

In tornado states, many people make it a hobby to chase twisters. Curious people try to get close enough to look at a tornado, watch its destruction, yet not get caught in its path. Sometimes we get too close; we even invite the whirlwind into our lives. We need to be on the alert for tiny little twisters that we think will "just make us a little busier for a while." We may like the tiny twisters because we like to be busy or because we like the attention a full life brings. Or we might be striving to reach a goal and think, "Oh, I can take on just one more project. I can handle it."

Take the Superman cape off, throw off the Wonder Woman gloves and vow to be on whirlwind alert! It may be that a hurricane is just offshore and you are so busy planning and preparing for your wonderful future that you have missed the warning broadcasts.

Other times, the weather looks fine from shore. You set sail on your plan. Suddenly the storm hits. You simply set out for a three-hour tour on the SS *Minnow*, but you wind up shipwrecked on what feels like a desert isle! (If things are bad enough, you may feel your only hope is to sell the royalty rights to your story and have another cheesy sitcom made of your life—like Gilligan!) But there is real hope for weathering the storm.

Weathering the Storm

In *The Scariest Place on Earth*, science writer David Fisher describes his attempts to prepare for Hurricane Andrew. He knew that hurricanes rotate counterclockwise and that the temperature rises as the barometer falls. He knew that the worst damage was north of the eye and that the safest place in the house was away from doors and windows. As the storm approached, though, he wished he had made better provisions. He was low on gas for the grill and low on batteries. He hadn't boarded up the sliding glass door or taken the fans off the roof.

> The roof was redone a few years ago, and at the time I installed two aluminum turbine fans. . . . They are guaranteed to withstand sixty-mile-an-hour winds; in a hurricane they are supposed to be taken down and the hole that is left in the roof battened over with a metal cover. I go up on the roof but find the attaching screws have rusted shut. . . . Nothing I can do will get them loose, and I leave them up there, spinning even now in a terribly weak breeze. Aside from the fans and the sliding glass doors, I think, we are in good shape. (Yes, but aside from that, Mrs. Lincoln, how'd you enjoy the show?)[4]

Later, Fisher describes his feelings during the height of the hurricane. "I check my watch. It's still running; somehow that surprises me. How can anything be normal in this maelstrom?"[5] How can anything be normal in your twisted circumstances? There is no "normal," but you can achieve a peaceful, hopeful, unique life—even if the hurricane rages. You and your marriage and your family can survive and even thrive.

In the following chapters we'll discuss *how*. By establishing priorities, choosing a workable life management option, creating a grid for technology and honing crucial success skills, you and your marriage and family can survive this hurricane of life. Above all, do not panic!

*   *   *

Time Out of the Tornado

At the end of each chapter, there is an exercise to draw the two of you together. Often, in the middle of the tornado, it is the little things, the small gestures of love, that get lost or set aside. As you work through the big issues, remember the little things as well.

Whatever pressures you and your spouse are dealing with right now, *make contact!* The time-crunch tornado will tear you two apart, so right now, this moment, make contact by doing one of these three things:

1. Look up and wink. Wink and smile. Small things go a long way when you are in a tornado of time pressures.

2. Call your spouse at work. Don't talk long; just say "I love you and I wanted you to know."

3. Give a squeeze—a hug, a holding of a hand, a gentle pat. Remember to touch in a tornado!

Part I
SUCCESS
SKILLS

2

LISTENING

*Y*ou haven't heard a word I've been saying!" shouted Jeannie.

"What are you talking about?" returned Blake with obvious frustration in his voice. "We've been talking for over an hour, and you think I haven't been listening? I just think you are being too emotional!"

"How would you know if I am emotional? You haven't ever heard one single beat of my heart," Jeannie blurted out, knowing her words would inflame the conversation. "I thought you were special, but you really are just like any other man. How can I ever trust you if you won't listen to me?"

"Whoa! You are really hurt about this, aren't you?" responded Blake, desperately looking for some way to turn this conversation around. "I thought I was trying hard to talk to you more."

"You have been *talking* to me more. You just haven't been *listening!*"

Listen to Key Words and Phrases

Blake and Jeannie are stuck at a point where many couples find themselves. They are spending quite a bit of time talking to each other, but they seem to be getting nowhere in their relationship. They don't know how to listen in a way that creates intimacy. The reason for this is that we are all subtle communicators. We throw out hints rather than boldly telling our spouses how we are doing. As we learn to respond to these "hints," we can encourage our spouse to reveal more of what is really going on in his or her heart.

People reveal themselves in stages. They start out with "safe" statements and progressively share more risky and vulnerable truths if the atmosphere of the conversation is conducive.

So a key principle in promoting intimacy is *permission.* If your spouse senses permission to share more without being judged or prematurely "fixed," new information will be shared. This new information will lead you to a better understanding of what your spouse is all about at the emotional level of his or her life that motivates actions and decisions. Here are some ways to grant permission to your spouse:

1. Repeat the key words or phrases your spouse says, with a warm voice inflection that says, "I have heard what you said and am ready to listen to more."

2. After your spouse has been talking for a few minutes with your encouragement, summarize what you have heard and then ask, "Is that what you have been saying?"

3. After a significant amount of sharing, when you think you have a good idea of what is motivating your spouse, describe a time in your life when you think you have felt the same way. When you are done describing this event, ask your spouse, "Is that what it is like for you?"

There are some common tactics that are thought to be useful but which actually disrupt the process of intimacy:

1. Avoid saying "I know just how you feel" and "I understand what you are feeling." This is an impossibility. For instance, I (Bill) will never understand what it is like to be a woman because I am not a woman. I will never know the tension of putting my career on hold for eleven years while waiting for my kids to start school. The only way I can relate to these influences in my wife's life is to listen to Pam and let her explain to me what it is like to be Pam.

2. Avoid asking, "Why do you feel this way?" The answer is, "I don't

know." Our emotions have never had the ability to think. We feel what we feel because of past influences and developmental factors. Emotions are not rational in their makeup, and so they don't think before they express themselves. The goal in intimate conversation with your spouse is not to analyze emotions and come up with some kind of solution that will make your spouse never feel this way again. The goal is simply to grow a little closer and reaffirm your love. This love you share with your spouse can be worn down over time. If you are not careful to reaffirm it often, it loses its vitality and can be swallowed up in life. When, on the other hand, you maintain the habit of often reestablishing the bond of love that drew you together, you can experience a growing joy with each other. And that is better than "finding a solution."

3. Don't try to fix your spouse. Your husband may say, "I am often intimidated by my boss." Do not respond with, "There is no reason to be intimidated. You are bright, intelligent and talented. Your boss is just threatened by how good you are. Be brave, honey. It will be all right!" In doing so, you shut him down. Your husband is probably trying to get a conversation started with you that is bigger than work. It probably has to do with his lack of confidence or lack of understanding of how competition works in an adult world. Or he may be contemplating a job change and be checking to see how accepting you may be of having that conversation. Or he may be intimidated by you, and he is trying to lead into the conversation by talking about his boss first! Whatever the case may be, you will never know if you attempt to fix him rather than let him work through the process of healing with your listening help.

"Let's try again," Blake said, reaching out and holding Jeannie's hands in a way that said, "You're safe with me." "You mentioned that I don't listen; tell me what you mean by that."

"I tell you how I *feel,* and you just tell me how I should *act,* " Jeannie cautiously said.

"So I just tell you how you should act?" Blake responded with a reassuring curiosity in his voice.

"Blake, when you tell me what to do as if it is a simple thing, you make me feel stupid." Jeannie was hesitatingly becoming more vulnerable.

"I make you feel stupid?" Blake asked with genuine surprise in his voice. He had always thought Jeannie was one of the brightest people he had ever met. Her statement made him feel pity and anger at the same time, both of which he swallowed for her sake.

She sensed his genuine concern and was amazed at herself when she blurted out, "You make me feel the same way my parents used to, when they told me I was an accident and they wished I'd never been born."

"They told you that?" Blake's astonishment was obvious to Jeannie. They had been married for five years, and Blake had never heard about this before.

"I was sixteen. I couldn't believe it when my dad said it first. We were having this really big fight. I was being pretty difficult, I admit, but I don't think I deserved that. I looked at my mom and asked if it was true that I was an accident—that I was unwanted. When she just looked down at the ground in silence, I felt my heart fall through my feet. I've tried hard to cover up my pain all these years, but it keeps coming back to haunt me. Whenever you treat me like I don't know what I'm doing, I feel that same pain again."

"I am sorry, Jeannie. I didn't know."

"I know you didn't. And I try to tell myself that you don't mean to make me feel this way—but sometimes it just overwhelms me. I didn't know whether to tell you or just be angry with you to protect myself."

As Blake embraced Jeannie, he marveled at the new sense of warmth and trust in their relationship. He saw that night that he would be wise if he learned how to listen more.

Listen to Your Irritations

"Whenever you do that, I get so frustrated!" shouted Gene.

"Whenever I do what?" inquired Betsy with surprised indignation in her voice.

"Whenever you go on and on about all those people you help. You care about so many people and their problems. I just can't handle it. I am tired of hearing about all this stuff!"

"Gene, what is going on? I never knew this upset you. I always thought you liked my sensitivity."

"Well, I used to. I mean I do. Oh, I don't know what I mean. It just makes me mad," Gene admitted knowing that he was off base but not knowing why he was upset. For some reason, he couldn't just give it up.

Gene got his introduction to the intimacy of irritation. You see, Gene had been attracted to Betsy by her sensitivity. She seemed to care so much about him when they were dating and during the early years of their marriage. She seemed to be wrapped up in his life and his needs. He was so flattered by the attention and so impressed by her insight that he became jealous when she cared too much about other people instead of just him. He wanted to keep the benefits of her sensitivity for himself rather than sharing them with other people. As she became more concerned about the needs of those around her and focused less on him exclusively, he felt a growing agony in his heart.

The challenge in Gene's heart is to learn that the very thing he loves most in Betsy is the thing that irritates him most. This is a very common scenario. You married your spouse because being together addressed significant needs in your life. You felt special, more complete. As a result, you were drawn close enough to take the big step of commitment and become husband and wife. But then the things you loved about your spouse appeared to change.

Perhaps the strong convictions your wife had about doing the right thing made you feel you could trust her. But now they are becoming an irritation when she turns them on you and your behavior. Or the concern your husband showed for your emotions and your well-being early in your relationship is threatening when you see him showing the same concern to others. Or the strong masculinity of your groom that makes you feel safe and secure can also make you feel lonely and isolated because he doesn't talk with you the way you wished. Whatever you appreciate most about your spouse could be the point of highest irritation!

If you listen to these irritations and are willing to look beyond your anger to the qualities in your spouse that are so vital to your own life, you will find you can build your marriage even as you struggle. Your irritations can be the springboard to new conversations of intimacy with your spouse.

To turn your irritations into insights, try the following:

1. Make a list of the characteristics you appreciate most about your spouse. Keep this list in a place where you can review it often. Reminding yourself that you love your spouse is one of the best ways we know of to lasso the whirlwind of modern life.

2. When you begin to get angry, ask yourself, "What did my spouse say or do that has got me so upset?" Something was done that triggered strong emotions in your soul. These strong emotions can either be seeds of anger or bridges of intimacy. If you can identify the trigger event, you will be close to turning it to your advantage.

3. Ask yourself, "What positive quality in my spouse's life is this irritation related to?"

4. Repeat to yourself at least seven times, "I love my spouse for . . ." inserting the positive quality in your spouse's life that attracted you in the first place.

Listen to Your Passwords

Every couple gets in conversational binds from time to time. We all have sensitive emotional needs which we have trouble managing. And these lead most couples to develop patterns of communication that are counterproductive to the growth of their marriage. When a couple gets stuck in these patterns or an emotional need sidetracks a conversation, it can be recaptured by a *password*. Passwords are words or phrases the two of you agree on that help you get back on track. They can be humorous or nostalgic statements that have special meaning to both of you. They remind you that this relationship is important and that you are committed to making it work. A password will break the ice of a stalemated conversation, because you have agreed ahead of time that it will.

Blake and Jeannie learned that one of their greatest obstacles to marital intimacy was the habit Blake had of trying to fix Jeannie. She would share her concerns about various aspects of their life, and Blake would jump in and offer "microwaved" solutions. When he did this, she felt put down and heard the messages from her past that she wasn't good enough. This became destructive to their marriage as she shifted into self-protection mode to fight off the perceived onslaught from Blake. They talked about a password they could use to remind them they really loved each other and wanted to connect.

Their solution was a stroke of genius. They both loved the program *Home Improvement* and connected it with laughter and hope. So they decided on the following password: "It looks like Tim Taylor has his toolbox out again." Jeannie had Blake's permission to use this anytime she felt Blake was trying to fix her. If she felt the feelings of low self-esteem or anger coming to the surface, she could lovingly look into Blake's eyes and use their password. This would cause Blake to stop and think about the effect he was having on his wife. Blake also had permission to use this phrase when he sensed he was trying to fix the situation and he saw that Jeannie was feeling run over in the process. He might just say, "Uh-oh, am I being Tim Taylor again?"

Since they started using the password, there has been more laughter in their home, but there has also been a greater degree of understanding between them. They now feel they have a way to interrupt conversations that had been going awry and to steer them in a healthy direction. They no longer sit around after an argument wondering what happened.

The danger of passwords is the temptation to manipulate your spouse. If one of you is upset, the other might be tempted to use the password to force your spouse to be "more reasonable" and "see things my way." You may also be tempted to throw this password up in his or her face, to end conversations that are unpleasant but necessary to the health of your marriage. These passwords must be used with compassion and an honest desire to build a healthier relationship.

Recently, I (Bill) found a way to handle a situation that has been irritating to me for years. I am a one-task-at-a-time man who likes to start a project and finish it before I begin another. As a result, I tend not to entertain too many ideas. I feel the need to pursue most of the ideas I have to see if they have potential. The only way I can realistically do this is to limit the number of ideas I let myself juggle. When I feel myself getting overwhelmed with the responsibility of my life, I take a break from new ideas. This helps me relax and prepare for the next round of responsibility.

Pam, on the other hand, is an idea person. She pumps out ideas like sunshine. I am constantly amazed at the unceasing flow of ideas that comes out of her mouth. I have come to realize that Pam relaxes by coming up with and discussing new ideas. She uses new ideas to relieve stress. It is as if she escapes the heaviness of responsibility by discussing what could be rather than dwelling on what is. This has the effect of energizing her and getting her prepared to ride out the next wave of responsibility.

This pattern in our life has been a source of significant irritation. Often, when we are sitting around relaxing, Pam will begin sharing her growing list of inspirational ideas about how to make the world a better place to live. As I listen to what seems to be an endless stream of ideas, I find myself getting worn out. I didn't understand it for a while. It seemed strange to me that this would be such an irritation, since I genuinely like trying new experiences. I finally realized that I was getting overwhelmed because I felt I needed to act on every one of these ideas. If they had been my ideas, I would not have shared them until I was ready to create some action. I assumed Pam was operating the same way. But she wasn't! She seems to develop an overload of ideas. Talking about them helps her weed through them to decide which ideas should be adopted and which are just good discussion topics.

When I realized this, I asked Pam if it was true. "Do you think I should take every idea you share with me seriously?"

"Well, of *course* I do," Pam responded indignantly.

"No, what I mean is, should I think that I need to act on every idea you bring up, or are some of your ideas just for discussion?"

"Oh, a lot of the ideas I bring up are just for discussion."

"So you don't feel the need to carry out all those ideas you bring up?"

"Of course not! I could never do all those things."

"Then why do you bring them up?"

"It's the only way I can get them off my mind. When I freely talk about my ideas, the ones I need to act on keep coming up. The ones I need to let go of just go away."

That was when the light went on for me. For the first time in fifteen years of marriage, I realized I didn't have to feel responsible for every idea Pam came up with. When we were newlyweds, it was flattering to me to be able to take her ideas and make them happen. After we had children, it got harder. By the time we landed in the middle of a complete list of adult responsibilities, it was downright impossible. Now it was as if a big weight had been taken off my shoulders. I asked Pam, "When you are sharing ideas that I really don't want to act on, can I just say, 'Pam, that is a great idea!'?"

You can't imagine my relief when she said, "I think *that* is a great idea!"

"That is a great idea" has become a password that carries a great deal of meaning for us. Whenever one of us uses this phrase, it makes us laugh, but it also is a compliment to the creativity and ambition that we both appreciate about each other. I have found a new way to appreciate Pam in an area that used to leave me feeling I could never keep up with her demands.

Looking for a way out of the miscommunication whirlwind? Try listening.

"That's a great idea!"

*   *   *

Time Out of the Tornado

Right now, ask your mate, "How was your day?" Listen. Don't say anything. Just listen. Give a reaffirming smile, nod your head, make eye contact, but don't say a word. Don't think about what you are going to say next; just *listen*.

3

FORGIVENESS

*H*ow could you do this?" Peter asked Kari angrily. "I can't believe you could get involved with another man. I thought you loved me."

"It isn't like we had sex!" Kari defended. "All I had was a friendship that helped me feel important. You had a much bigger problem with pornography."

"Why can't you let that go? It happened five years ago!" added Peter with noticeable agony in his voice. "Are you going to keep hanging it over my head? Every time we disagree about anything, it always comes back to the same thing!"

The whirlwind of too much responsibility and too little time, the storm of unforeseen problems and financial ruin, the hurricane of personal illness and the raging tornado of technology—they all whirl above us. You may be tempted to "run for cover" to activities or relationships that threaten your marriage. These diversions may be as simple as a critical attitude that wears down your mate or as complicated as an affair or sexual addiction. Then, to the degree that your relationship has been hurt, trust needs to be rebuilt.

"I don't think I can trust you now," Peter pointed out to Kari, thinking he was the most injured party.

"I haven't been able to trust you for the last five years," Kari said with tears in her eyes. "When I found those magazines and tapes in your closet, I felt sick. When you got angry at me for finding them, something in me went numb. I have been looking for clues that say I can trust you again, but I keep coming up empty."

"I am sorry, Kari. I never meant to hurt you. I just got overwhelmed with life, and the escape into the magazines seemed to help—at least for a little while. Will you ever be able to forgive me?"

Peter's apology and request for forgiveness had a noticeable effect on Kari. She felt some of the hurt dissolve, and she found a new willingness, even desire, to be close to Peter. Over the next few days she noticed that hope for a renewed relationship with Peter was growing. They both knew it would be an uphill battle, but they had taken the first step.

Shut Out Bitterness
It's not hopeless! Rebuilding relationships is not easy, but it can be done. There are no quick fixes, but there is a starting line. Forgiveness is the first step on the road to recovering intimacy, whether the hurt is big or small. It is the key that unlocks the door to give your marriage a second chance.

There is a lot of confusion over what forgiveness is. Forgiving is not sweeping your pain under the rug and pretending it never happened. It is not just burying your emotions to placate the other person. It is not forgetting or acting as if you have forgotten. Forgiving is not saying "It doesn't matter," as if there were no standards of right and wrong.

Forgiving someone is a private act—a decision you make within your own heart, not dependent on the response or attitude of the other person. It is a decision on your part that the actions of another will not ruin your life. Forgiving means cleansing your heart of bitterness, leaving the offending person in God's hands and simply letting go.

Forgiveness is often confused with reconciliation. Whereas forgiveness is a private matter, reconciliation is an agreement made between two people to put a relationship back together. Reconciliation takes two. In the process of reconciling after the friendship has been violated, an opportunity is granted to begin again. Reconciliation begins with forgiveness. The offended party first extends to the other the forgiveness that has been resolved internally. Then the couple begins the process of developing healthy skills that build trust and growth in their marriage.

Forgiveness is easier to accomplish when there is realistic hope of reconciliation. That is what Kari experienced when Peter asked for her forgiveness. The hope that Peter still cared for her and his own remorse over what he had done gave Kari courage to release her own hurt. But even if reconciliation is not on the horizon, each of us must forgive to prevent bitterness and unhealthy thought processes from ruining us.

In our ministry, we have tried to pattern forgiveness after Christ and his ultimate act of forgiveness on the cross. To give "forgiveness handles" that you can grasp in a practical way, we have come up with six statements that provide a working definition.

1. I forgive _____ (name the person) for
_____ (name the offense).

It is important to specifically name the offense. Vagueness in dealing with forgiveness only leads to doubts about whether forgiveness has truly been achieved.

The greatest example of forgiveness in the world is the forgiveness Jesus Christ has offered us. He has granted freedom from guilt to each of us who will trust him. This is indeed good news! But the good news starts with a very tough reality. "All have sinned and fall short of the glory of God" (Rom 3:23).

Too often we skip this step. Maybe it is because you think your hurt feelings are your problem. Maybe you are upset by what your spouse did, but you think people have the right to do whatever brings them happiness. Maybe it is because you are afraid to bring up pains from the past. Or maybe it is because you just don't know how. If you are looking for a clear path of freedom, get specific.

Peter and Kari have actually started well, even though it was difficult to face one another. Kari had stopped trusting Peter because he was defending his own shortcomings rather than admitting them. Over time, her heart wandered and she began engaging in conversation with a coworker who met many of her needs. To get the process of forgiveness started they both got specific.

"God, I forgive Kari for letting her heart wander toward another man," Peter said bravely in prayer.

"God, I forgive Peter for foolishly letting pornography capture his heart rather than coming to me," Kari weakly conceded.

2. I admit that _____ (name the offense) was wrong.

The apostle Paul increases the seriousness of forgiveness in Romans 6:23 when he writes, "The wages of sin is death." Paul understands forgiveness to be a life-and-death issue that begins with the honest confession of something done wrong. In our politically correct world, we often feel uncomfortable saying something was wrong. We may feel we are being critical or judmental. But if nothing wrong had been done, there would be nothing to forgive (and no problems in relationships). If the goal is forgiveness with the hope of reconciliation, you aren't being a critic or a judge—you are taking courageous steps of love.

"I admit that Peter's attraction to pornography was wrong." As Kari said these words she felt a strange sense of strength. Recognizing this as Peter's problem rather than her own calmed the uneasy feeling within her that somehow this was her fault.

"I admit that Kari's relationship with her coworker was wrong," said Peter with a sigh.

3. I do not expect _____ (name the person) to make up for what he (she) has done.

Too often in life, we expect the person who hurt us to come back, apologize profusely and beg our forgiveness. It would be ideal if this happened, but it is rarely the case. Even if the person does ask our forgiveness—and maybe offers a gift to try to make up for the offense—the offense is still not erased. Nothing, absolutely nothing can ever undo what was done. Once an offense is committed, *it cannot be uncommitted.* So we need to let the person off the hook.

If we hold on to the demand that the offender make up for the wrong, we put our personal growth on hold as we sit around waiting for the phone to ring. By letting him or her off the hook, you are not saying that the offense is any less wrong. Nor are you saying that there will be no consequences. By not expecting the person to make up for the offense, you are turning the right to revenge over to God. You are trusting that *God* will hold the person accountable. You give up the right to be the hangman.

The real tragedy in not forgiving shows up here. If you refuse to let the one who hurt you off the hook, you give him or her control of your life. Too many people withhold forgiveness until they receive an apology. As you are waiting, the one who hurt you is going on with life without a thought about how you are doing. As you repeatedly feel the pain, you pay the price for your victimization over and over again. There is no need to allow the one who hurt you to have further victory over your life. Don't wait! Get that person out of the loop of your emotional life. Even a person who is no longer in your life and who will never know about the forgiveness has this power over you until you forgive—and let go.

As Peter and Kari courageously took responsibility for their own responses to one another, the process of discovery expanded. Peter decided not to expect Kari to ignore every other man she met, and Kari decided to stop waiting for Peter to prove that he wasn't hiding pornography. In the process, Peter came to grips with his hatred toward his parents for their influence on his self-esteem. He realized he was sabotaging his marriage because of his own struggle with guilt. Kari found the strength to admit that she had been molested by her uncle as a young teenager. All men were suspect as a result, and Peter's transgression was all the worse because of it.

4. I will not use _____ (name the offense) to define who _____ (name the person) is.

When you define people by the negative impact they have had on your life, you make them bigger than life. You certainly have made this person bigger than you, because you have given him or her the ability to determine the state of your life. Kari used to think, "My uncle ruined my life when he molested me. I will never have a normal life. I will never be normal." In holding on to this, she made her uncle bigger than herself. He became, in her mind, the monster who destroyed her. When she found Peter's pornography, she assumed Peter was just like her uncle, and her love all but died. But the truth is, her uncle is merely a sinner who needs to be transformed by the grace of God. By recognizing this truth, she was able to see that he was no bigger than herself. He didn't have more power. He didn't have more insight. He didn't have more importance than she did. This shrank her uncle down to size and gave her the hope that she could grow out from under his controlling influence.

Then comes the step of forgiving yourself for the things you have done. This step is vital. When you define yourself by the things you have done wrong, you encourage a process of decay. It has been well established that we live out what we think about ourselves. If you think you deserve an unhealthy life, you will live out an unhealthy life. If you think you deserve to be punished, you will live out a self-destructive life. If you think you are a failure, you will avoid the path of success. If, on the other hand, you define yourself as the object of God's grace and an adopted child who is in line for God's favor, you will pursue healthy avenues of growth and development.

5. I will not manipulate _____ (name the person)
with this offense.

Manipulation is an attempt to emotionally blackmail another person. It is an attempt to protect yourself from the influence another
person has had on you. There is something in the human spirit that
believes we can control another's influence through manipulation.
The tragedy is that every act of manipulation confirms that the one
who hurt you still has control of your life! Your very approach to life
shows that you are still afraid of what this person might do to you,
so you control the behavior of others in an attempt to feel powerful.
You run in an endless circle of self-protection, never enjoying the
freedom of truly living.

Jesus does not constantly bring up our past sins to force us to do
his will. Rather, he calls us to walk with him as new creatures who
have been set free from the past and our mistakes. We are encouraged
to live as saints rather than as recovering sinners. This does not mean
God ignores the influence of our past. He has committed himself to
helping us grow through our past and reach up to a whole new life.
We would be wise to look forward to the life ahead of us rather than
constantly try to overcome the past that is behind us.

6. I will not allow _____ (name the offense) to stop
my personal growth.

This is probably the most important step. Too often we allow the
sinful offenses of others to dictate the course of our life. It is almost
as if we think we are punishing the ones who hurt us by refusing to
pull our lives together. Or we are emotionally committed to keeping
things the way they have historically been in our families. If our
ancestors were bitter, then we are bitter. If our ancestors were prone
to depression, then we are prone to depression. This applies to everything from alcoholism to anger to lack of confidence.

Peter was told by his parents throughout his childhood that he would never amount to anything. Whenever he accomplished anything of significance he was told, "You may be smart in school, but your room is a mess and that shows your true character. You may have done well in sports, but you don't even know how to organize your life. You don't have what it takes to really be anything." Peter heard the message loud and clear.

Peter responded to the barrage of insults and votes of no confidence by determining in his heart that he would prove his parents wrong. He set out frantically to accomplish enough to show his parents that he was somebody—that he was important. He became a workaholic at a very early age. His goal was to prove his parents wrong.

But there was also a desire within Peter to have parents who were right. As a result, Peter found himself falling short in most of his pursuits. The word that characterized his life was "almost." He almost got straight A's in school, falling short by one B. He almost got a scholarship to play college athletics. He almost won championships and he almost ran a successful business. It seemed he always stopped short of being truly successful because he couldn't get beyond the message of his family.

In his early thirties, Peter began to discover that his lack of success was linked to his lack of forgiveness of his parents. He was harboring silent bitterness against the influence of his past. He realized also that he was almost a great husband. He was kind and sensitive, but he sprinkled his relationship with Kari with land mines such as irresponsibility over his schedule and the use of pornography. As he walked through these six statements of forgiveness, he realized he had allowed his approach to life to be shaped by the mixed messages of his parents. He was locked into overworking and undersucceeding as a pattern of life. He had to decide that he would no longer let this counterproductive programming rule his life.

Peeling Off the Layers

Peter is still working on this by honestly walking through the layers of forgiveness. Over and over again he walked through the process of forgiving his parents for the things they had said. He initially felt better, but after a few months he found himself upset again with his parents and unable to get away from the anger he felt toward them. He thought at first that he hadn't really forgiven them. But as he talked with Kari, he realized he was now upset because of his own lack of confidence, caused by the discouraging messages. He was mad at his parents not for what they had done but for what they had developed in him.

He walked through these same steps with his lack of confidence. He found a new freedom in his life for a few more months, until he found himself fighting depression because he seemed to be afraid of new opportunities in his life. He came to realize that his lack of confidence had made him afraid to try new ventures and pursue new ideas—he was afraid he would miserably fail. He had not been aware of this fear because he wasn't trying new ideas. He was overcommitted to ventures he was comfortable with and ignoring the new opportunities that would fill out his life.

He found another layer in the process of forgiving his parents. He found himself ill-equipped for the challenges of adult life and he was blaming his parents. As he let his parents off the hook and chose to push his own personal growth, he began experiencing a growing sense of courage in competing in an adult world.

Peter and Kari were amazed at how their courage in forgiving each other had opened up other areas of forgiveness that were actually more influential in their lives. They saw that forgiveness is not just a one-time event but a pattern of life that gives birth to more life. They have since found a new joy in their daily interaction as they have committed themselves to keeping short accounts.

*   *   *

Time Out of the Tornado

Stop! Think of a mistake you have made for which your spouse has forgiven you. Buy a card and write in it a thank-you note for the grace that you have experienced. You do not need to mention the specific incident, but you might say something like "Thank you for accepting me just as I am," or "Thank you for being there for me even when I don't deserve it," or "It is a joy to be married to someone who looks at life as God does." Don't forget to express appreciation for your spouse's forgiveness, even while you are in the tornado.

4
SIMPLIFYING

*A*n *exodus followed the whirlwind* of economic slowdown that hit southern California. Couples went elsewhere in search of the American Dream. Some found it—some did not.

Terrell and Chelsea were tired of the hectic schedule caused by Terrell's daily commute. That was tiring enough, but when Terrell got home, he had to go to work at his second job.

"We just couldn't make it on one income!" remembers Chelsea. "We had four kids! Two were still toddlers, and we had committed ourselves to be the main providers of their care. Besides, even if I did work, nearly all the money would have just gone to day care anyway. We loved California, but owning a home here and providing for the needs of our family was killing us!"

Terrell and Chelsea moved to the Pacific Northwest, as did Jeff and Chris, Bob and Trisha, Jim and Maggie, and Grant and Teresa—all friends from the same neighborhood. However, three years later, half of those couples are looking for a way to move back.

"We thought it was the schedule, the circumstances, the house," Chelsea proclaimed over lunch on a recent house-hunting trip to southern California. "It wasn't. The pace of life was in *us!* Life in this little town of a hundred is driving us crazier than the house payments were. We realized that we can live more simply—even in California. We were overburdened in California. We'd never take on such heavy financial obligations again. But the kids are all in school now, so maybe I can help provide this time. Terrell and I are determined to find a workable plan and move back!"

Ken and Mindy, on the other hand, love the life they've found in Mindy's small midwestern hometown. "We love it here." says Mindy. "We can actually make it on one income! Neither of us finished college, and the job market in the city we were from was paying nearly identically to the job market here—only housing costs are about a third of what they were in the city! We just bought a home here for $60,000, and a home like this in the city was over $200,000. We could have never owned a home if we had stayed. I wanted the kids to have a sidewalk that was safe to ride their bikes on and a backyard to play in. To move up in the job market, one or both of us would have had to get a lot more education, and we didn't have the resources—or the desire—to do that."

"We are very aware of the tradeoffs," adds Ken. "We really miss our church. There was always something going on in the Christian community in the city. Resources and events were always readily available. Everything is slower here—but you get used to it."

Is Your Life Simple Enough?
Modern couples wrestle with the question *Do we run away to someplace simpler, or do we simplify the life we have and stay put?* Before you pack up the bags and rent the moving truck, consider these red flags, or warning signs, of a life that has become too complex. Remember, you can't run away from yourself. If the problem of simplicity is a set of attitudes or beliefs you hold, the path to a simpler life will be found in you, not in a new location.

Red Flag #1: The Tempo of Life Is Too Fast
Are you running from one activity to another? Do you miss the days

when you sat around after an activity enjoying conversation and reveling in its success? Are you tired of being late to events because you are squeezing so much into one day?

Then your activities are too numerous. For a family to function best, a natural rhythm or pace has to form. In long-distance bicycle riding, each rider has a natural tempo that can be maintained almost indefinitely. Going faster or slower than the tempo causes the rider stress. Too fast a tempo and the rider exhausts his or her resources. The loss of energy can cause the rider to lose focus, resulting in possible injury or failure to complete the race. A tempo that is too slow is hard on the body but even more tedious to the mind. The rider feels held back and may give up hope.

Each individual has a pace. Couples and families also have a pace. You may have a personal pace that is quicker than that of the rest of your family. That's okay as long as you learn ways to go at your pace without ignoring your family's needs. On a bike trip, the person with the quickest tempo rides in front of the other cyclists. The riders are sheltered from the force of the wind and can actually speed up their tempo because there is less resistance.

For a group to ride together, different individuals take turns being the lead rider and wind breaker, because the job can get exhausting. The others then "draft" behind, almost being pulled along by the tempo of the group. Families can function this way. Different members can take responsibility for a variety of tasks; then the rest can just fall in line and draft behind their energy. Bicyclists who ride in a group and draft in this way can outdistance individual riders.

You and your spouse are in the race of life, going for the distance. Your family is a group that needs to find its own pace. You may ride out front for a while; you can even sprint out ahead, then come back, check on the rest and ride with them for a while, then do that all over again. The key is to communicate the pace.

I (Pam) prefer a quicker pace of life than Bill. We are both busy—but I like it. When Bill gets busy, he looks for ways to slow the pace. I look for ways to draft so I can keep going. However, we both enjoy rest stops! I can keep going at a quick pace as long as I can see a rest-stop sign and know rest is coming. Bill and I divide up our life responsibilities. Sometimes he provides wind resistance for me as I ride behind. Sometimes I pick up the pace and shelter him from the wind so he can take a breather.

A couple needs to find the pace of life that is most healthy for their marriage and family. Some couples thrive on the easy, carefree, no-rush, no-schedule, drop-by neighbors, low-key lifestyle. Others prefer a life that has ready access to cultural events, business contacts and resources, and lots of people. These couples like to squeeze the most out of every waking moment. Relaxing to them is not taking a nap; relaxing means going out and doing something!

Most couples fall in the middle somewhere. They want resources and events but also peace and quiet. They want to reach their individual potential but not if the cost is an insane schedule. Good bicyclists will keep a steady pace both up and down hills. They do this by shifting gears. As the landscape of your life changes, shift gears so you can maintain as steady a pace as possible, and you'll make it. Rest stop ahead.

Red Flag #2: The Cost of Living Is Too High

Too much month left at the end of your money? Are you getting creditors calling your home or work? Do you depend on credit to get through each month? Your life may cost too much.

It is easy in our world to set our budget by the standard of living of our friends, relatives and neighbors rather than by our income. A bankrupt man once told C. H. Spurgeon he was ruined by a new sofa. "That sofa was a bad beginning. It was too fine for me. It made my old table and chairs look awful, so I bought new ones. Then the curtains had to be replaced. The furniture in the rest of the house was sold to correspond to the new things we had purchased. Then the house was not good enough for the new furniture, so we moved to a larger one. Now, here I am bankrupt."

It is easy to fall into the trap of discontent. New things are not wrong, but buying new things when you do not have the means—or even the potential means—is a disaster waiting to happen. A couple needs to take a good look at their financial potential. How much education and job experience do you have? How savvy are you in regard to credit and consumer loans? What assets do you possess? Keep your spending in line with your skill level and earning potential.

Several couples we know earn large incomes but have very limited knowledge in handling money matters. They have chosen a very simple pay-cash-for-everything lifestyle. Others we know have smaller incomes but sophisticated financial skills. They often use credit cards with benefits, such as frequent flier miles or accrual toward the purchase of a car, but pay off the balance each month to avoid the huge interest rate. With them, timing is everything; they stay right on top of their accounts to take full advantage of each buying and saving situation. The key is to be a good steward of the money God entrusts to you.

Your skill level in money matters should match the pace of life at which you live. For example, if you are both very busy and have a hard time getting to the bill bin every month to write the checks, then you'll need a simple financial system. However, if your life and career are less demanding, you might be able to handle a more complex monetary system, because you have time to plan and account for all your spending and purchases.

What Does a Second Career Cost?

Before you run out and work harder so you can buy more, consider the hidden costs of a second income. Below is a sample of costs that can greatly reduce the financial benefits of working more. These figures will vary a lot. Plug your own family's estimates into the grid.

Per Month

Child Care

  Infant care: $400
  Preschool for one child (early/late care extra): $450
  Home day care for one child: $320 to $720

After-school care for first to sixth grade: $100 to $200
Example: Caleb = $360; Brock and Zach = $300: total $660

Transportation

Extra gas, wear-and-tear on car: $50 to $100
Second car (purchase price plus insurance and maintenance): ?

Additional clothing for working parent:

$20 to $100, depending on job requirements

Food

More fast food and prepared foods: twice a week at $20 per time
for family of five: $160
Lunches out: average of four a week at $5: $80

Job obligations

Cards and gifts for coworkers; professional dues;
subscriptions to journals): ?
Taxes (approximately 20 percent of new income): ?

Extras

Cleaning service (depending on frequency): $60 to $200
Lawn care: $30 to $100
Technology (pager/car phone): $10 to $200

*   *   *

Example of monthly expenses for family of five:

Child care for 3:	$660
Transportation:	$100
Clothing:	$25
Meals:	$240
Office:	$10
Extras:	$100
Taxes:	$400

Total: $1535

The cost of a second income for this family of five would be a minimum of $1535 per month, or $18,420 per year. That means that the net income would need to be *much higher* in order to allow any headway financially. Then there are the additional factors of lifestyle changes, child care, time spent (or not spent) as a couple. In this example, earning $2100 in a second job outside the home is equivalent to earning $600 by working from home or cutting expenses by $600. Only you can decide which is easier and more beneficial to your marriage and family.

Red Flag #3: Your Ambition Is Too Grand

Ambition can be a good thing. It gets us out of bed each morning. It gives us the desire to do our best at whatever task is ahead. But blind ambition can be a cruel taskmaster, driving you past your personal limit and beyond your ability to cope with life. Chasing the almighty dollar or the next promotion can drive a person to the point of collapse and can ruin an otherwise heathy marriage.

Ask yourself these questions: Does this desire match Scripture? Does it match my ability to achieve it? Does this desire allow me a stress level that I can handle? Does it transcend my decision-making ability? Does it fall well within my skill level?

Yes, God can stretch you and help you grow. But God usually stretches people in small increments. God doesn't send you out to fail. Often we are just in a hurry and don't want to earn our way to the top. We just want it handed to us on a silver platter.

It is the process of day in and day out service and decision-making that brings spiritual advancement. The forging of our character day after day prepares us for more responsibility.

Red Flag #4: You Have Too Many Material Possessions

Is your car a disaster area? Can you never keep up on housework? Is the grass a foot high? When things break, do you have no time to fix them and no money to hire the job out? Can you only halfway shut your closet doors and no longer actually park your car in the garage?

If all your answers are yes, you don't own your things; your things own you. Everything you possess can possess you. Material possessions are necessary, but they are also demanding. How much stuff do you really need?

For example, how big a house do you *need* (not *want*)? How much do you need to spend at Christmas (not: how much do you feel obligated to spend)? How many clothes are there in a necessary wardrobe (not a desired wardrobe)?

Try these exercises:

1. You are a pioneer in the Old West. You can take only what will fit in two covered wagons. What will be left behind?

2. You are moving to the mission field. Each barrel you ship costs an amazing amount to send. The dishes and kitchen equipment fill one barrel. Pack everything else for the house in one barrel, and then allow one barrel per family member. (The barrels are the size of a large trash barrel, not a dumpster or truck!) What would stay and what would go?

3. Consider the phrase *Everything you own costs*. Think about cutting your possessions in half. Would that be workable? Could you still keep your family running with half the possessions?

This is a painful area in our life. Several years ago, God got our attention by using a beat-up 1960-something Volkswagen bus. We wanted a van as a second car because we live so close to the beach and it's a blast to pile a bunch of people in with boogie boards, surfboards and food and head out to the surf for a few hours. A van would also come in handy as we were finishing our house and planning some yard and garden projects.

Well, we were given a van!

It didn't run. It desperately needed a paint job, but Bill thought that fixing it up would be a great project for him and the boys to do together. Eventually, our eldest could be the proud owner of a cool surf van. What dreams!

After hours, days, months of work, Bill did get the van running—kind of. The van was still looking really ugly, but it had a rebuilt engine in it, so we took it on a family vacation.

To make a long and very painful story short, we spent the first three days of vacation broken down, far from home, watching Bill work on the van. God graciously provided contact with some amazingly loving longtime friends who took us in, fed us, housed us and gave us pep talks. We never got the van working, but we did arrange to borrow a car, finish our vacation, then tow the van back home . . . where it sat for over a year. Finally Bill called up a parts yard, and they came and hauled it away.

It took a year because Bill had to part with his dream of having a restored VW bus like the ones seen at car shows. He had to come to grips with the very real fact that his career and our ministry life gave him no time for restoring cars. He watched sadly as the VW bus fell to the bottom of the priority pile. That bus is a symbol of our realization that we needed to pare down and simplify our life in order to obediently achieve the plan God has for us.

Red Flag #5: You Feel Unable to Give

Are you frustrated because you cannot give as much money as you would like to the causes you think are important? Do you wish you could give more to your local church? Have you felt empty because you couldn't help someone in need? Do you feel, at the same time, a pressure to increase your standard of living with each increase in pay?

One man committed himself to God to give a certain percentage of his income as long as he lived. From his first week's pay he gave $1 to the Lord. Soon his weekly offering had increased to $10. As time went on, he continued to prosper. Before long he was giving $100 a week, then $200, and in time $500 a week. This process started out as an intense joy, as he felt his hard work was making life better for many people. But after a while he found himself in conflict. He began to think that it was, after all, his money, and that he shouldn't be giving away so much. Finally he called a close friend.

"You remember the promise I made to God years ago? How can I get released? When I made the promise, I only had to give a dollar, but now it's $500. I can't afford to give away money like that."

His wise friend said, "I'm afraid you cannot get a release from the promise, but there is something we can do. We can kneel down and ask God to shrink your income so that you can afford to give a dollar again."

Seek to live a life that enables you to give to others and to the causes you believe in. Money is a cruel master. If it dominates your decisions in life, you may find yourself struggling with discontent, jealousy or simply the continual search for more wealth or possessions. If, on the other hand, you are able to discipline your financial life so that you can give, you will find joy and freedom.

Red Flag #6: Your Emotional Needs Are Unrealistic

Do you struggle when you have to leave the house in a mess? Does your appearance always have to be perfect? Do you struggle with ongoing anger or fear that keeps you from the peaceful life you desire? Are some of your reactions to problems or circumstances over-blown? Are you having a difficult time trusting others even though they've never given you a reason for mistrusting them?

We can simplify our lives by *letting go of our right to be hurt*. Bill and I decided early not to sweat the small stuff in our marriage. If he says something that hurts my feelings but I know it was by accident, I just forgive him and go on. I don't even bring it up for discussion. I know Bill is for me, so I function on that level. I really don't have the time or energy to "talk out" everything that I take wrong. Sometimes I take things wrong because I wasn't paying close enough attention—or sometimes it's PMS!

Most couples can also find more hours in the day if they *address the unresolved baggage* that drains off their efficiency. For example, Sally felt tired and sluggish. Everything in life seemed to be a major ordeal. Just making breakfast for the children exhausted her. She wasn't ane-mic or ill; she was depressed. She was convinced that her husband compared her with other women and considered her inferior. She felt she couldn't do anything right. But Sally's perception was not in line with reality. Her husband thought she was great-looking and fun to be with. He was growing weary, however, with this battle of trying to encourage a chronically depressed wife.

Sally came in for counseling. Years of baggage and abuse tumbled out. Unresolved issues from her past had been stopping her from having the future she desired. As she began to deal with the past, her present life (and that of her husband) began to be a lot less unhappy.

Emotional baggage from your past or within your marriage will eat up valuable time. It is like dragging around a hundred-pound weight all the time. It slows you down! Your brain is preoccupied or fuzzy. Making simple decisions is a chore. A drowning person can't go and rescue someone else. It's hard enough just keeping from going under. Often we don't excel in business, in community leadership or in our ministry because too much time is taken up with raking the compost piles of our lives. Instead of dealing with the garbage, we just want to rearrange it. Or we look for a distraction so that the garbage will not be as noticeable. Garbage is still garbage—it needs to be dumped out and hauled off!

If you seem to have the ability to function well in life but then have an emotional meltdown, there is probably something triggering that response. Take time to invest in yourself and in your marriage. Get the emotional help you need to get well. A wise pastor or qualified counselor can be very helpful as you try to discover what areas need to be addressed and healed. You and your family don't have time for denial. Get the help you need to get better and get on with life!

*   *   *

Time Out of the Tornado
Whoa! Pretend the house is on fire. Other than your family, what one price-less possession of your spouse's would you run to save? Take a minute and share why you would want to save that particular item. Then tell each other which of your own possessions you would want saved and why. Seal the story with a kiss.

5
TRANSITIONS

I'm not the same woman you married!" Janet screamed at Andrew.

"No kidding!" retorted Andrew. "The woman I married wanted to be with me. She wanted the same things as I did for the children. She had the same dreams I had. We wanted the same future."

"No; I didn't have any dreams of my own, so I just went along with yours. And they're good dreams, but I have some of my own now too. Why is it so hard for you to let me grow?"

"You're not growing. You're running away!"

"No, I'm not! I still love you. I still love the kids. All I want is to have a few hours a week free to use my gifts. I need to spread my wings and fly a little. I'll still fly right back to you and the kids. I love you! Oh, why does this have to be so hard?"

"I guess I miss you—that's all. And I miss our life. Back then I knew what to expect."

"Expect us to both grow and change, Andrew. Please just expect us to both change. I'll love you through the changes; will you love me?"

Encouraging Growth

If both of you expect change in your own development and in your marriage, you may be able to reduce the force of this whirlwind. Sometimes couples are caught off guard by the transitions of life, instead of expecting them and planning for them. A transition hits, and they get angry. Couples tend to be quick to pin the blame for the whirlwind on each other.

Let us emphasize this right now: It's not you! It's not your spouse! It's life! Life transitions can be demanding. Too often couples hang blame around the neck of the other when their conflict is actually a symptom of a natural life transition.

On page 57 you will find a chart of normal life transitions. Notice how most of marital life is spent in the trenches. Life is demanding! Between the birth of the first child and the empty nest there are definitely whirlwind years.

Marriages generally start on a high. Newlyweds think nothing could ever make them fight. Other people have conflict, but it will never happen to them—their love is different!

Then reality hits. Sometimes it's on the honeymoon. Sometimes it's later in the first year. But sooner or later, opposing expectations will collide. After all, marriage is like merging two rushing rivers together. Both may be going in the same direction, but there's going to be some turbulent white water where they mix.

Reality for most couples hits with the coming of the first child— whether "too soon" or according to plan, the little one changes Mom and Dad's life forever.

Or reality may hit in the unsuccessful struggle to have a child. For many couples, infertility is the first bitter pill that has to be swallowed. It is natural to want to place blame and find out whose fault it is. But even after you know the medical cause, there is no point in placing blame. If your marriage is to survive through this major stress, it will do so because you are a united team. The couples we've seen come through with stronger marriages—some eventually with children, some without—have all sought wise and varied medical advice. They have also plugged into support groups that specialize in infertility and surrounded themselves with friends who will cheer them on and en-

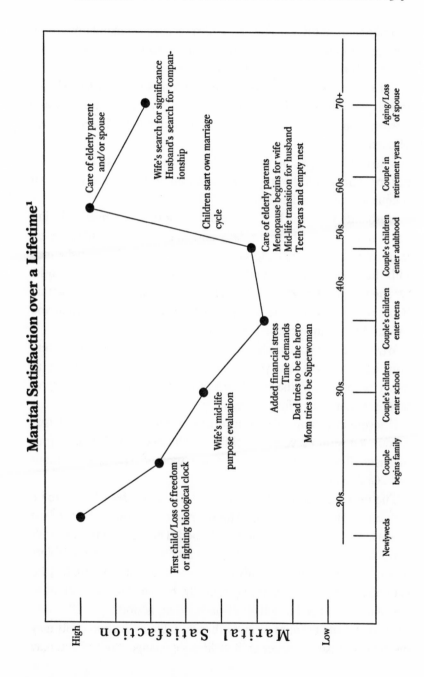

Marital Satisfaction over a Lifetime[1]

Marital Satisfaction

High — Low

Newlyweds | Couple begins family | Couple's children enter school | Couple's children enter teens | Couple's children enter adulthood | Couple in retirement years | Aging/Loss of spouse

20s · 30s · 40s · 50s · 60s · 70+

First child/Loss of freedom or fighting biological clock

Wife's mid-life purpose evaluation

Added financial stress
Time demands
Dad tries to be the hero
Mom tries to be Superwoman

Care of elderly parents
Menopause begins for wife
Mid-life transition for husband
Teen years and empty nest

Children start own marriage cycle

Wife's search for significance
Husband's search for companionship

Care of elderly parent and/or spouse

courage their marriage. They have also focused on maintaining spiritual growth and involvement in a ministry, so that the focus of life isn't totally on themselves and their problem.

For couples with a first baby, reality becomes sleeping less, changing diapers day and night, walking the floors with a crying baby and reworking the checkbook to try to find money for still another box of diapers.

Marriage changes here. It has to. Another life has entered the picture, and often several more children follow, each with their unique joys and challenges.

Husbands, your wife isn't purposefully ignoring your needs. She just has a body that is changing daily and hormones that change even more. She may be battling to stay in reality! She may be overwhelmed with the awesome responsibility of bringing new life into the world. Or she may just be exhausted. Grab some pregnancy and postpartum books on the day she finds out she's pregnant. Learn as much as you can, and hang on and love her unconditionally!

Wives, include your husband as much as possible: give him attention; let him know how you are feeling. Nurture your marriage as much as you can. Verbalize when you feel you can't meet the expectations you once had for your marriage.

If severe or prolonged conflict arises or if your intimate life hasn't rebounded within a year of a child's birth, seek help. Invest in your marriage. Resist the urge to blame one another. This is a strenuous time. Grab a lifeline.

The next transition early in marriage is that Dad feels he has to be Superman. He goes into overachiever mode and tries to be the best at work, the best at home, the best in bed. The Best Everywhere! It's as if a big S for Superman is painted on his chest. As the responsibility of a new family weighs heavily on his shoulders and (inevitably) he is unable to handle everything perfectly, he may take a moment to reevaluate and ask himself if all he is doing is worth the effort. As early as the late twenties or early thirties, a life evaluation crisis may hit: he may desire a career shift or lifestyle change. Both of you may feel exhausted. But hang on to each other; it will get better.

Women at Mid-Life

The mid-life transition usually hits a woman somewhere between her late twenties and late thirties, often at a time when her children no longer need her as much. The woman turns her attention outward and asks, "What's next?" In mid-life, a woman may also view her marriage as stale and her husband as inattentive. The couple has now been married just long enough to take each other for granted. "It isn't that they hate each other; it isn't that they don't love each other. They are just apathetic. They are bored, bored, bored."[2]

She may want to go back to school or to a career, or she may dream of starting a business of her own. She's looking for an identity apart from her husband and children. It's not that she loves them less; she just knows that she has to find the space in the world that is uniquely hers. She wants to develop her gifts and talents, if she hasn't done so yet—or she may feel the need to go in search of her gifts and talents.

Since we were aware that Pam would probably experience a mid-life transition in her late twenties, we were able to make a potential disaster feel more like a nerve-wracking roller-coaster ride. We had a lot of ups, because Pam discovered a whole new set of gifts and drives in her heart. I (Bill) watched as Pam developed a strength I had not seen in the first ten years of our marriage. But there were also a lot of quick turns and unexpected free falls that made both of us angry and frustrated. I had known that both Pam and I would experience mid-life reevaluations, but experiencing it firsthand was still difficult.

I (Bill) especially struggled with the free falls. I have affectionately referred to this transition in Pam's life as "The Awakening." Up until that time, Pam seemed to be content with taking care of the boys and me, along with assisting in ministry alongside of me. Now she was seeking her own place in God's plan. My response was to get angry. I felt hurt that she had not consulted with me first before sprouting wings and flying!

I was threatened because her newfound interests seemed to make her less interested in addressing our daily needs. By far the hardest part was her lack of interest in my opinions. I felt as if my comments did not matter anymore to Pam. She was chasing her dream, and I felt left out. It took me a year to work through my own feelings. I knew intellectually that Pam was going through a transition, but emotionally it felt as if I was being rejected. I had to remind myself that God was leading Pam in this and she needed my support, not my criticism.

I (Pam) too felt I was on a roller coaster. I was experiencing a growth in my skills as a leader, writer and speaker. I had a new vision of how God could use me outside the home. But at the same time, I felt my heart being tugged back home to Bill and the boys. My primary responsibilities were still at home, but I was frustrated with the daily mundane tasks. I knew our family was complete and soon all the boys would be in school. I loved work and ministry, and I loved my family. Anytime the two conflicted, I got the same feeling in the pit of my stomach that I get when a roller coaster plunges toward the ground. *Am I going to make this turn? Am I going to stay on God's track for me?* I wanted to. My love for and commitment to God, Bill and the boys kept me securely seatbelted to my convictions as I raced toward discovering more of God's plan for me.

I breathed a sigh of relief, as did Bill, when the two of us finally talked the problem through and hammered out a workable plan. It was like the comforting announcement at the end of a thrilling but unpredictable amusement-park ride: "Please stay seated until you have come to a full and complete stop." The ride was over—but Bill and I are anticipating other adventures ahead. There are always transitions.

The Trauma of Teenagers
In the midst of the wife's and husband's mid-life transitions, the kids go through the strange and wonderful metamorphosis called puberty. Hormones are raging and development is progressing at light speed as our teens seek out their own identity. Having teenagers in your

home is both an exciting and an aggravating time.

When children are young they need directives and commands. As they grow, they need direction and coaching in the development of wisdom. Teens need to be guided to make their own decisions in life; parents maintain veto power to provide protection while these future adults discover the reality of life. If teens are not given enough freedom in decision-making, they will be tempted to rebel. If they are given too much freedom, they may make decisions that are self-destructive or short-sighted. Couples often argue over where the line is, and that causes friction in the marriage in addition to the friction with the child.

This is a challenging transition because we must change the skills we use in raising our kids. We can no longer take total responsibility for our children and meet all their needs. We must, instead, teach our kids to take responsibility for themselves and release them one step at a time to live their own lives. This is a good time to read books on how to parent teenagers. And seek out mentors who have already been through it and who are willing to talk with you about what works. It is also a good time to reevaluate your schedule, because teens take time and energy. If you are already living a fast-paced life, teens may push you to the ragged edge. Small crises look much bigger when you're functioning on too little sleep, so do yourself and your marriage a favor: put some extra time into your schedule as a buffer.

Men at Mid-Life

Men hit their mid-life transition at a most inopportune time. During this challenging transition, a man is reevaluating his life and struggling with his identity and mortality. Mom may be in menopause, and the kids may be in their teens or leaving the nest! In some families, the care of aging parents lands during this stage too. Everyone just goes into survival mode! Every family member barely has time to deal with his or her own needs. But a wise husband, feeling the tug of midlife restlessness, will keep his focus clearly on his family. And a wise wife will turn her eyes to her husband.

Jim and Sally Conway, mid-life counseling specialists, advise women whose husbands are in mid-life crisis to remember, "he wants his wife to be a girlfriend and a lover, not just a mother and a household manager."[3] Sally also suggests, "Be your husband's best friend. Understand what he's going through and attempt to meet his needs. In other words be fun and sexy not naggy or bossy."[4]

Sally describes how she personally handled Jim's crisis. "I began to think in terms of how a younger woman would act around him. I decided to look at him with the eyes of a twenty-two-year-old and tell him what I saw in him and how I felt about him. I wanted to affirm him more and act more flirtatious."[5]

It doesn't do any good to blame the husband at this point—or demand he go back to the way he was! Walk with him through it, and your marriage will grow closer. You have the opportunity to fall back in love with him and he with you.

The Empty Nest

Marital satisfaction begins to rise again in most homes as the children launch out into their own lives. If a couple has built memories through all the struggles instead of placing blame, they will feel closer. Men tend to turn their hearts to relationships at this point in life. That hard-driving man may turn into a teddy bear. The wife may be asking, "How do I want to spend the remainder of my time?" If she didn't develop her uniqueness back in her twenties and thirties, this transition may be a little harder on her.

For couples who married young and whose children are starting on their own journey, this can be a second honeymoon time. They have less responsibility. The husband's heart is drawn home. And they have more financial security and earning power with fewer expenses. Retirement follows with its adjustments. Couples who investigate new horizons will have the opportunity to fall in love all over again.

Because many families have boomerang kids (who move out, then move back home), these years can include an extra transition. If grandparents are called upon to raise their own grandchildren, they will experience again their children's transitions, but this time with more wisdom. The positive side of this rerun is that they won't be traversing the rough terrain of their own transitions at the same time! Everyone comes out better if boomerang kids are made to be responsible for their own lives. If grandparents are asked to raise grandchildren, then they need the authority and not just the responsibility.

Old Age

Unfortunately, old age eventually robs us of our health. Marital satisfaction is again challenged as health fails. Caring for a terminally ill spouse and then watching his or her death can be the ultimate challenge during these years.

We may be tempted to deny we are aging. But denial taken too far can be dangerous. Women who avoid their pap tests and mammograms are risking their lives. Men who avoid crucial health exams such as prostate testing can be gambling with years of their life. General Norman Schwartzkopf is the national spokesman for prostate cancer survival. He says there are two things men fear: incontinence and impotence. His response to men who refuse the prostate test for fear of impotence: "You are never more impotent then when you are dead." Taking steps to maintain and guard good health is a loving response. Your spouse would like to keep you around.

When I (Pam) was a young girl, each Friday I would go to the nursing home with my grandmother. I'd hand out fruit and tissues and sit and chat with the patients or sing or dance. There was one couple, in their late eighties, who always sat and held hands and patted each other as they talked. They were still in love. Later, as newlyweds, Bill and I would often sit at church near a couple who had been married over sixty years. We loved to see him reach over and squeeze her hand. She would respond with a wink. It was so wonderful to see that the glimmer never has to go away. If the doors that threaten marriage are shut, the whirlwind will fade and become the gentle breeze of comfortable, tender love.

This Is Only a Test!

"This is a test. For the next sixty seconds this station will be conducting a test of the emergency broadcast system. This is only a test." Then the radio blares that shrill, annoying tone. As we each navigate through the transitions in our lives, we may periodically run our own "test." Our behaviors at these times may be just as annoying and inconvenient as the radio's screech. Your spouse will look at you and ask, "Do you still love me? Even at this new stage?" Sometimes we will test our love for one another, even though we know intellectually that there should be no need. When the test comes, you may be tempted to turn off the test signal and run away from your spouse. But your lover needs reassurance that you care now more than ever.

A husband at mid-life may ask you to join him on one of his adventures. You may feel you would look silly; you may think you're too old. But if the request is not illegal or immoral, try it. A wife may ask a husband to sacrifice time away from the sports channel to accompany her on a business errand or to a new art class. The husband may feel it is inconvenient, but if he goes with her, he will be investing in a brighter future. No matter the stage, spouses seek reassurance from each other. We know what is important to our mate, but we want to know if we are more important. Sometimes knowingly, sometimes subconsciously, we will test our mate, to see if he or she *really* cares. When this happens to you, know that it isn't a lifestyle change—it's only a test.

The first test I gave Bill was on the last night of our honeymoon. After a fun night out at a dinner concert, we came back to the hotel and had a wonderfully intimate time. It was well after midnight. We had a flight out the next morning at six to visit relatives for Christmas. But I wasn't tired. I was excited. Everyone was going to meet my wonderful new gorgeous husband!

I chatted about everything I could think of. Then I started running out of conversation. So I recounted for Bill every boyfriend I'd ever had since kindergarten! I thought he'd want to be filled in on these important details of my life. Well, predictably, he kept falling asleep.

I kept waking him and saying outrageous things like "Don't you love me? Don't you want to spend time with me?" (This is now an example of what I tell young brides *not* to do on their honeymoon!)

Then, as if that wasn't bad enough, I began serenading him with all the country tunes I'd been raised with on the farm. My L.A. boy was a very good sport but very tired at this point. Finally I couldn't remember any more twangy lyrics, so I said, "Bill, I guess we should go to sleep. We'll get a few hours in!" He showed wonderful restraint and said, "Yeah, Pam, I think we should." He gave me a kiss and rolled over. The next morning in the car I apologized for keeping him up so late. He just said, "I really do love you, Pam. When I fall asleep, it's not because I'm not interested; it's because I'm tired." He could have lashed out and said something true but unkind like "Who would be interested in a bad rendition of Tammy Wynette at two a.m.?" But he didn't! He definitely passed the test!

Tests, transitions, tornadoes. With each transition, whether it is turbulent or smooth, there is opportunity for growth, both as an individual and as a couple.

*   *   *

Time Out of the Tornado

Push *Pause!* Send your lover a high-tech message. Write in the space below what note of love you will send ASAP by e-mail, fax, or voice mail. Include something you appreciate about your mate that wasn't evident in him or her when you married.

6
GOAL
SETTING

*T*humbing through a positive thinking catalog, Bill and I ran across a plaque that read: "Some men dream of great accomplishments, while others stay awake and get them done." That is the purpose of a goal—to get things done. A goal is *a dream with a deadline.*[1] A goal is a tool to get the two of you where you want to go. A goal makes hope a reality. We want to suggest that you set some goals for yourselves individually and for your marriage from this point on.

Dream On, Baby!
In order to set goals, you have to know what your dreams are. So, the first step is for each of you to complete the following exercise.

Write a story describing the "perfect" life. In the story address material, financial, emotional and spiritual wishes. (Money is not a limitation in this story; try to describe what monetary level is acceptable for the hopes and dreams you have for your marriage and family.) Write only about three paragraphs; then read your stories aloud to one another. What were the common denominators? What skills do you need to develop to achieve the dream? Underline those that are "portable"—that could be achieved anywhere at any time. Now underline the most important idea in each story and compare your values. Place an asterisk next to the dreams and desires that have eternal value. (God says people and the Bible are the top two eternal priorities.) This will give you some idea of where to begin setting your goals as a couple and a family.

Before accepting the position of our current pastorate, Bill and I made a list of what we wanted in our next location. I (Pam) wanted a city close to a university so I could finish a degree. Bill wanted a university town too, for the options of pursuing a Ph.D. and/or teaching at the college level. It would be icing on the cake if the community offered a variety of youth activities, outdoor recreation and cultural amenities. We wanted basic expenses to be low enough to be met by one salary. We wanted a safe neighborhood with a good elementary school, and we wanted to be within a day's driving distance from at least part of our extended family so that a few holidays could be spent together.

We also made a list of qualities we desired in a church that would make a good fit. We took a good hard look at ourselves and asked, *Where can we best serve?* We had a heart for the city, and God had both equipped us and burdened us for the fast-paced southern California lifestyle.

The move to San Diego met most of the expectations. However, the housing costs were amazingly high. So we adapted our goals and built a home with sweat equity. (However, we would probably never do the building again. You can do that only when you are young and able to burn the candle at both ends!)

Your list may be different—and your desires may change—but the biblical principles that lay the foundation for life will remain constant. For example, an affordable home may look entirely different in various parts of the world. In some places wealth is a one-room flat; in other places it is a mansion with a pool. For example, when we decided that building a home was the best stewardship of the housing money God had graciously given, our main goal was to create an "average" home that those with less income and those with more could both feel comfortable visiting. Our guiding principles were to (1) not be a stumbling block and (2) be "like" those we were trying to reach. No matter where God moves us in this life, those principles will be part of the grid we use to evaluate the choices before us.

To keep our future options broad and portable, we have chosen to write and speak, because both skills are highly portable—we could essentially live anywhere. And both skills are appreciated in academic and church settings. We also are pursuing further education because that will keep our options open. Our desire is to have timeless principles guide the constantly changing choices that must be made day in and day out. Having portable skills that can flex with the call of God will give you the ability to make more confident choices.

A Mission Statement

Another tool that has helped us set goals is our marriage mission statement. (Most couples have one, but many have never written it down.)

When you were dating, what were the things you said you'd like to see God achieve through your marriage? Bill and I wanted to live our life in such a way that others, seeing our marriage, would want to know our God. Our marriage was priority one from the very beginning. Along with that priority, we also had a commitment to individual discipleship—to equipping others in their faith and helping them introduce people to Jesus Christ. We had a desire to have a family characterized by inner stability, open communication, respect, trust and love. Lower on the list of priorities was our desire to stay physically active throughout life. Our material desires were even lower on our list of goals, because we treasured experiences more than possessions. (We'd rather kayak down a river than buy a new sofa.)

When you share the same priorities, it is easier to write a mission statement and much easier to write achievable, specific goals. Our mission statement is:

We, Bill and Pam Farrel, have a desire to fulfill the Great Commission through using our skills in professional ministry and by being committed to personal discipleship as a lifestyle. We want our home to be an oasis where those who enter can see Christ at work in our marriage and family and where they can find hope. We, the Farrels, are committed to fun and friendships. We value people more than things. We prefer memories over material goods. We are committed to raise our children in such a way that they will have the opportunity to know the benefits of personally knowing Jesus and walking with him. We are committed to helping them discover their talents and equipping them to help fulfill the Great Commission and to have fun and a fulfilling life while doing so.

Based on this mission statement (which was only oral for several years) we could set goals in a variety of areas. We chose to set long-term goals (seven to ten years), then short-term goals (three to five years), followed by yearly goals.

An Important STEP

In order to maintain a balanced life, it is helpful to write goals in four major life areas. Write goals that will help you take another **STEP** forward. You'll want to develop

Your **S**piritual Life

Your **T**eam

Your **E**nergy

Your **P**roductivity

Spiritual life: This area includes goals that build a closer walk with God—for example, a daily personal devotional time with God, Bible studies, church attendance, verses you'd like to memorize, and growth activities such as retreats, conferences, Christian radio and books you'd like to read. When you are connected to God, your perspective is renewed and your decision-making skills sharpen because you will be thinking more like God.

Team: Included in this section are goals that will build into your significant relationships, like marriage, family and close personal friends. One author recommends that we prioritize our lives by who will cry at our funeral.[2] When you maintain healthy relationships, then you will have more emotional stability to tackle life. Your motivation for life will increase as your relationships are strengthened.

Energy: To maintain a high level of energy, you must carefully manage the areas of life that are of importance to you as an individual. These will include your personal finances, emotional well-being, physical health and social life. It will also include those activities that are less urgent but still vital to you as an individual—your hobbies, study, sports, reading, leisure activities.

Productivity: This area includes goals in your career, education and ministry (both public and personal). What type of work do you want to pursue? What position do you want to attain in that field? What type of education do you need to fulfill these pursuits? Who are the people you would like to personally influence for Christ? How would you like to use your gifts in your local church ministry?

Goals in a Suitcase

Goal-setting in this whirlwind of a world has become much more difficult. Goals are usually linear. In a world as fast-paced as ours, goals require much more flexibility, or they can become a trap! For example: By twenty, we'll marry; by twenty-five we'll buy a home; by thirty we'll begin a family; by forty we'll have climbed the corporate ladder far enough to buy a bigger home. Then a pool; then pay for our kids' college education; then retire in ease and comfort. Ahh! The American Dream!

The American Dream has become the American Nightmare. In an environment of corporate downsizing, constantly shifting markets and an unstable economy, modern couples need an abundance of portable skills in order to accomplish their linear goals. The key word in today's world is *change!* Goals should be set to build into you, your spouse and your family values that will survive constant and rapid change. Flexibility and adaptability are the key components of goals today and in the future.

With persistence, dreams can be achieved by gathering portable skills that will help you anticipate and navigate change.

Robert Barner, in an article in *Futurist* magazine, explains that "the career strategist . . . will not chart a rigid career path toward a single long-term goal [but] . . . will keep . . . planning flexible."[3]

There are four key survival skills to keep in mind when setting goals, particularly in connection with your careers.

1. Environmental scanning refers to the ability to tap into computer and personal networks to continually benchmark one's skills. Being "on-line" and well networked will prevent technological obsolescence and help you gauge the current market value of your skills. You will also gain the ability to identify potential employers and fast-breaking employment opportunities.

2. Portable skills are skills that can be easily transferred to other work environments, such as knowledge of standard financial software, project management or total quality improvement tools. Contextual skills, in contrast, are those relatively nontransferable skills based on knowledge of a specific organization's work procedures and processes. *Portable* means you can pick up and carry your talents and skills and apply them anywhere at any time.

3. Self-management is the ability to manage one's work either when alone or within the context of a management-coached or self-directed work team. The worker of the future needs to be self-motivated and not wait around for someone to tell him or her what to do.

4. Communication skills include both face-to-face and written communication tools, essential to job survival as teams become increasingly geographically dispersed and culturally diverse. The ability to communicate clearly and consistently within high-stress, time-limited situations will be critical.[4] The office of tomorrow may be nonexistent, replaced instead with a talented team scattered across the globe and connected via phone, fax, modem and the Internet.

Having skills like these is like being a military family. Greg and Beth are one couple we know who take their family values with them wherever they are assigned, whether stateside or abroad. Their purchases are made according to what is easily moved. Greg and Beth have job skills that can be put to use in a variety of career situations. No, we don't all have to move every six to eighteen months, but we should work on developing our skills in such a way that circumstantial change has minimal effect on our goals.

How to Write a Goal

As you do a first draft of the goals that will help you get to your dreams, keep these three things in mind.

1. Goals must be specific. How will you know you've fulfilled a dream unless you can articulate what that dream looks like? For example, a nonspecific goal would be *I'd like to be happy.* Well, what makes you happy? What are you like when you are happy? Is happiness something that God wants you to set as a goal?

A better example might be this: *I'd like our family to have an income that would adequately supply our housing, food and basic lifestyle desires.* You could then list those desires and estimated costs to come up with a target income need. After that you could brainstorm on how to meet that income need and decide if meeting the need is worth the required lifestyle. Can you find ways to increase your income to hit your target? If earning that amount is too great a strain, you might adapt the list, look for a less expensive location or look at other lifestyle changes.

2. Goals must be realistic. I cannot write a goal that I cannot control. For example, I can't say, "I wish I were taller." I (Pam) am five foot four, whether I like it or not. My height is beyond my control. So getting taller is not a goal I should set. And I can't say, "I wish my husband were more romantic." I can't control my husband. (I can provide opportunities for relaxed romance and openly communicate my romantic desires and feelings, but I can't *make* him be romantic, so this is not a goal I should set.)

3. Goals must be achievable with God's help. We want to set goals that are just beyond our power to achieve, because these goals stretch us and make our faith grow. Each speaking engagement that comes in for Bill and me is a faith builder. We can only let people know the topics and seminars in our portfolio; we really believe God fills our speaking slate. We can't make anyone invite us in.

In business, all you can do is be persistent at working your plan, then trust that God will work behind the scenes to make the connections you can't make. In matters with your children, your goal is to be an excellent, compassionate parent, but all parents realize that you can't protect your child twenty-four hours a day; you have to trust that God will be with them.

But I Hate Goals!

Sometimes people feel overwhelmed by the goal-setting process. Goal-setting may feel to you like being asked to paint the Empire State Building with a toothbrush. But it doesn't have to be that overwhelming. Think of goal-setting like climbing stairs. You want to get to the top and each stair (goal) helps you get there.

Other times people feel they can't obey God and at the same time set goals. Somehow they feel they are usurping his control or direction. That is impossible! We are not in control of our futures. There are always variables we cannot control. But we are *stewards* of our futures. Psalm 90:12 should be our prayer: "Teach us to number our days aright, that we may gain a heart of wisdom." And Ephesians 5:15-16 advises us, "Be very careful, then, how you live—not as unwise but as wise, making the most of every opportunity." The key is flexibility—ranking our will under God's will. We set goals with the attitude, "This is our educated guess at life. God, if you want it changed, we know you'll make it very clear!" The commands of God found in the Bible are an expression of his goals for us. Often he leaves the application of the goals up to us.

Sometimes one spouse likes setting goals while the other drags his or her feet. That can be manageable with a good attitude. Bill likes the concept of goal-setting, but early on I discovered he didn't like the process of writing out his or our goals. So I interviewed him. Each year, usually as we travel on family vacation, Bill and I talk about goals and review where we are and where we're going. I play vice president and record the conversation in the form of written goals. Then, because I'm not fond of spreadsheets, Bill takes the goals and writes financial objectives that need to be accomplished to fund the goals. After this process, we sit down and reevaluate the goals, make scheduling adjustments, discard goals or place some in a "not now, but in the future" file. We try to work as teammates, each using our strengths to benefit our team.

If you both hate goals, use the format below. Simply fill in the blanks to create a goal game plan. Do this exercise at first as a one-year plan; once you get the hang of setting yearly goals, you can progress to short-term ones (three to five years), then long-term ones (seven to ten years).

Spiritual Life Goals
Husband:
To grow in my walk with God this year, I'd like to spend _____ hours per week reading/studying the Bible. The study I choose is:

I will pray _____ (minutes/hours) per day. The time I will use to pray is:

I will meet my need for fellowship by attending (list a worship service and small group):

I will pray for an opportunity to share Christ with these people:

Other ways I'd like to use to grow are (maybe Bible memory, listening to Christian radio, meeting with a mentor, investing in magazines or Bible software):

Wife:
To grow in my walk with God this year, I'd like to spend _____ hours per week reading/studying the Bible. The study I choose is:

I will pray _____ (minutes/hours) per day. The time I will use to pray is:

I will meet my need for fellowship by attending (list a worship service and small group):

I will pray for an opportunity to share Christ with these people:

Other ways I'd like to use to grow are (maybe Bible memory, listening to Christian radio, meeting with a mentor, investing in magazines or Bible software):

How much will it cost to meet these goals? Go through your list and note any items that cost. For example: Do you need to purchase a Bible or Bible study guide? Do you want to get up-to-date information by subscribing to Christianity Online? Will you meet your mentor for breakfast each week? Calculate your yearly spending costs, then divide by twelve to get an average monthly cost for your spiritual growth goals. Try not to scrimp—you are investing in the most important relationship available to you!)

Team Goals
Husband:
My emotional needs:

Ways to meet those needs:

My sexual needs:

Ways and times to meet those needs:

My intellectual needs:

Ways to meet those needs:

Love list (ten things my wife could do that would say "I love you" to me):

Places I'd like to go on a date:

Wife:
My emotional needs:

Ways to meet those needs:

My sexual needs:

Ways and times to meet those needs:

My intellectual needs:

Ways to meet those needs:

Love list (ten things my husband could do that would say "I love you" to me):

Places I'd like to go on a date:

Now set goals for the place(s) where you will live.
Husband's top five:

Wife's top five:

How much will it cost to meet these goals?

Energy Goals
Husband:
My hobbies:

My physical needs (dentist, doctor visits, medications):

My social needs (club memberships, nights out with guys, favorite forms of entertainment):

My connections to extended family (phone bills, gifts, trips):

My parenting responsibilities (sports coach, homework helper, extra-curricular or volunteer leadership):

Wife:
My hobbies:

My physical needs (dentist, doctor visits, medications):

My social needs (club memberships, nights out with gals, favorite forms of entertainment):

My connections to extended family (phone bills, gifts, trips):

My parenting responsibilities (sports coach, homework helper, extra-curricular or volunteer leadership):

Productivity Goals
Career goals:
Husband:

Wife:

Can we both achieve these goals and keep the lifestyle we want?

Cost of career goals:

Educational goals:

Husband:

Wife:

Cost of the goals:

Public ministry goals (any positions held at church or in a parachurch ministry):

Husband:

Wife:

Personal ministry goals (any ministry you'd do even if you weren't a part of an organized group):

Husband:

Wife:

Cost of ministry goals:

(You may also choose to write goals in these four areas for your children or with your children.)

Now complete the budget worksheet. Then reevaluate to see whether you like the ramifications of the goals you've set. Is it a go, or do you need to adjust?

Monthly Budget Worksheet
Income
Salaries:

Other:

Total income:

Expenses
Tithe:

Taxes:

Housing (all expenses including rent or mortgage, insurance, upkeep, decorating, all utilities):

Groceries:

Auto (car payments, gas, upkeep, insurance, tax and license):

Insurance (life, health and any other insurance):

Debt (all debt excluding mortgage and monthly minimum payments):

Entertainment/recreation (eating out, tickets, video rental, any other activity, plus a monthly vacation savings amount):

Work expenses (child care costs; any professional expenses):

Clothing (list a monthly dollar figure for each family member):

Savings/retirement:

Medical expenses (any copayments, medical or dental bills not covered by insurance; monthly cost of prescriptions and over-the-counter medications):

Miscellaneous (personal care needs—haircuts, cosmetics, dry cleaning; personal allowance for each family member; unreimbursed ministry expenses; gifts; educational costs; hobbies; postage; photos; magazines and so on):

Total expenses:

Subtract expenses from income:

If income exceeds expenses, plan how to invest the surplus. If expenses exceed income, plan some quick action to cut expenses, raise income or both.

*   *   *

Time Out of the Tornado

Memo to yourself: *I will make it a goal to date my mate!* Now do it. Make a reservation, order tickets, call a sitter. Do not proceed until you have completed your date arrangement!

7

GOAL
COORDINATING

Y *ou think what* you *do* is so important! Well, what about me? What about *my* goals and dreams?" Sharon pleaded with Jeff.

"Yeah, yeah, yeah—I know, your work is important too! I never said it wasn't."

"You act like whatever I do is insignificant. Well, I'm great at what I do! Plus I'm the one who always stays home when the kids are sick— you, you always have an important meeting that you just can't miss. I have meetings too—but I miss them, because some things are more important."

"Hey, wait a minute, Sharon. Last week, I took Trevor to the doctor because you had to meet a client. You make it sound like I'm the world's worst dad." Jeff looked wounded. He had the same look as a punch-drunk fighter ready to go down for the count.

"Okay, you aren't a bad dad. I'll give you that. You just aren't here. And even when you are here you're not really *here*." Jeff knew Sharon was right. It seemed that during the past few years they both suffered from that dreaded preoccupation disease.

"Sharon, we can't keep going like this. I think what you do is valuable and significant. I know you feel the same way about what I do. We have both been robots around the kids. They talk to us, and we don't even acknowledge them until they wave their hands in front of our faces to see if we're still breathing. And I miss *us*. There is no *us* anymore." Jeff cautiously reached across the kitchen counter to touch Sharon's hand.

"I know. It feels like we're going in opposite directions. Sometimes it seems like a bad dream. It's like the Wizard of Oz gone mad. We can't get back to Kansas. We can't find the wizard to give us directions, and there's no yellow brick road to lead us out of this mess."

"Then we'll just have to make our own road. We'll get on the same path, even if we have to forge it ourselves."

She frowned. "It won't be easy."

"But it's got to happen! If we don't sit down and have a long heart-to-heart, we're going to lose each other in this whirlwind."

"I love you too much to lose you."

"Me too," he answered, looking directly into her eyes. "Are you up for this?"

"No, but that doesn't matter. We have to find the answer."

"Everything has to be up for discussion in both of our lives."

"And the kids' lives too." Sharon ran her long nails through her hair. She took a deep breath and a long sigh came out.

"What's that?"

"Oh, when things get rough, it just helps to sigh . . ." she giggled.

"At least that's a good sign."

"Yeah. Okay, I'll get some paper."

Jeff jumped up. "And I'll get the ice cream."

"Ice cream?"

"Life will look a little better with some chocolate!"

"I wish that's all it would take."

What It Takes

To get on the same page of life, you'll need to find out what is really important to each of you. Often arguments and misunderstandings develop because we assume we know what is important to one another. But priorities are deceptive. They shift around like the pea in the shell game. You don't want to be guessing when you dovetail your life together; you want to *know* what is important!

For a really long time, I assumed Bill's work around the house and yard was out of necessity. I thought he felt he had to mow the grass, fix the car and do home improvements because we couldn't afford to hire them out. When things got busy and the "Honey Do" list grew, I felt bad because Bill's precious few days off had to be spent around the house. Then we had "the talk."

Bill was working on finishing a project on our unfinished home. The younger boys needed closet doors hung in their room. Bill worked hard all day to finish the job before out-of-town company arrived. He came down and announced that they were done.

I ran upstairs and looked, gave him a hug, said thanks, and off I went. After about a half an hour of getting things ready for our guests, I realized I hadn't seen Bill, so I began looking for him. I knew he was done with the closets, but I couldn't find him. I checked the shower (a logical place to go after a dirty job and ten minutes before guests arrive). I looked in the garage, in the office, out in the yard, then I finally charged up the stairs. Bill was still standing in the exact place I'd left him thirty minutes before. He was gazing at his closet door creation!

"You're still here! Bill, they look terrific. What's wrong?"

"Nothing. It just feels so good to be done with something!" Bill exclaimed. "All day long, every day, I work with people. People are never done—at least, not this side of heaven. Those doors are done! They're *done!*"

Now I understood why Bill took so long to do each project. He wanted the project to be done well—and stay done! The list of chores that I thought were a cumbersome drag Bill sees as a gold mine. Those chores bring balance to his life. Bill is talented with landscaping and woodworking. He built the home we live in. What drives him crazy is that it isn't done! Now I know that Bill desires a portion of his time to be spent on what he calls "mindless work with my hands." He also has a high need to stay on task and get something *done!*

Both of you should take the quiz below—on your own. Rank each item 1, 2 or 3. A 1 means it is very important to you. You would keep your 1 activities even if you never could do a 2 or 3. A 2 means it is important—not a main focus, but you don't feel it can go undone. A 3 means if it gets done that's fine, but if it doesn't, no sweat. The 3's are those things that can drop out of life when things get hectic, or that can suffer a bit in quality and it doesn't make you crazy.

Life Responsibilities
_____ Being in good physical shape
_____ Having a neat, clean home
_____ Having your family finances in order
_____ Maintaining correspondence
_____ Having quality intimacy/romance
_____ Having time with your children (overseeing homework, team parenting, and so on)
_____ Having fun as a family (trips, vacations, kick-around time)
_____ Succeeding in your career
_____ Having a personal ministry/involvement in church
_____ Extracurricular activities (community involvement, career enhancement, philanthropic activities)
_____ Having a nice car(s)
_____ Furthering your education
_____ Achieving more financial success
_____ Time alone
_____ Time with God
_____ Time with mate (talking, relating nonsexually)
_____ Time for a hobby
_____ Other_____

Now compare your lists. Which things are ranked the same? Mark those with an *. You're probably less likely to argue over those areas. Circle the areas that have the greatest differences (like yours is a 1 and his is a 3!). You'll have to negotiate in these areas. They are hot spots.

List It All!
Now, take a set of 3 × 5 cards. List everything you are responsible for. Everything! List all the household chores and all your work responsibilities. If you run a business, list what it takes to make it run. List whatever time it takes to keep relationships running in your marriage; with your kids; with in-laws (or out-laws!). If it takes time, write it down! (Or order a *Priorities in the Whirlwind* organizing set from Masterful Living Ministries. The address is in the back of this book. Most of the work has been done for you!)

Now prioritize the cards. Rank them 1-3 again. Maybe both of you gave "having a neat, clean home" a 1 in the survey above, but one of you was thinking of the kitchen and the other had the bathrooms in mind. And "clean" means different things to different people. Bill and I found out early in our marriage that the bedroom and the living room needed to be neat for Pam to be happy. Bill had to have a clean kitchen with the dishes done and put away or he couldn't relax. We should take responsibility for that which is a high priority to us! So I (Pam) keep the house overall orderly and organized (at least on the surface!). As our life has picked up its pace, Bill has taken on the responsibility for the kitchen. He either does the dishes or delegates them to the boys, and he deep-cleans the kitchen regularly.

I am also responsible for the "emotional caretaking": our family heirlooms, photo albums, baby books, Christmas cards and letters to friends. Bill is responsible for de-junking our closets and our lives regularly—I am too sentimental. Everything reminds me of a story or a memory, so of course it's much too valuable to part with. However, I rarely miss what is tossed! The only rule is that Bill makes a "debatable bin" that I get to review before he tosses it out.

Another area of possible conflict will be those areas that you both marked as 3's but that are 1's in daily life. For example, neither Bill nor I love to do bills and finances. But whether we like it or not, bills have to be done! Bill was a math major and he's great at it, so he has taken it on. But I have pity on him and his sacrifice, so I usually bake him chocolate chip cookies and then sit down with him to sort out the bills or write out the checks or file—something to keep him company.

Sold to the Highest Bidder

Now the negotiating begins.

When I was a little girl, I played a parlor game called Pit. It was a mock version of the commodity trading that happens on the stock exchange. In Pit, players would try to gather all of one commodity, say, corn. They would trade other players for the commodity they prized most. One player might trade four wheat cards just to get two corns. That is exactly the kind of thing you'll need to do when you come to the negotiating table with your spouse. If something is really important to you, you'll have to compensate in other areas. The priority is to arrive at one dovetailed life. There is an art to leaving some things undone.

"I'll trade you child care on Mondays and Thursdays, if you'll do this stack of errands. I hate errands!" Bill exclaimed.

"That's fair. I need the time for ministry appointments and business errands, so these household errands will fit in. But since I'll be running back and forth, why don't I pick up the boys from school? That way you can stay home to work on the yard and do bills."

"That's workable. But who's going to take this stack of responsibilities?" Bill picked up the pile of 3's that neither of us wanted.

"Let's see. What's in it?"

"Laundry. Let's divide and conquer on that. If you sort it all on Monday, I'll wash and fold it the next few days; then Thursday you can oversee the boys as they put it away. Fair?"

"Fair. How about lunches?"

"The boys can make their own. Brock and Zach can each take responsibility for keeping a car clean this year too."

"Good idea. I'll take homework and the errands that come with it."

"Great. But I'll still set aside one day close to science fair time to help," said Bill.

"Of course. That's tradition now. How about this stack of ministry priorities?"

"Let's take those cards on our getaway and pray over them. We need to decide which to do now, which to have our new staff person do, and which are just great ideas for the future. Pam, you can easily fill your days with good things and not get to your writing. God has called you to that, so we have to help you get some boundaries on your life so you can do it."

I looked at my pile of 1's. Romance for Bill and me; the boys' activities, daily homework and bedtimes; writing; women's ministry; exercise. It would be tough to get all the 1's accomplished if I didn't set some boundaries and protect that time. I remembered the year Bill fought to get my attention. He missed me and wanted more time with me. That's how the cards all started. Bill and I both wanted more time together and we were having a tough time finding it. I smiled.

"What are you smiling about?" Bill asked.

"I'm just remembering how this got started."

"Desperation."

"Yeah. But it's all paying off. Every year it gets easier to negotiate responsibilities. There are fewer arguments between times—and, best of all, I really do have more time with you."

"Hey! Who's going to take the windows?"

We both pointed to each other. Shook our heads no.

"Back to the bargaining table."

There are only twenty-four hours in a day. As a team you have to come up with a workable plan on how to spend those hours. In most families resources are also limited, so you'll need a plan on how to save or spend those resources wisely. (For more help on the steward-ship of resources, contact Christian Financial Concepts, Ronald Blue & Co. or Crown Ministries. Addresses are on p. 177.)

Bill had started noticing that his exercise time was getting shorter and shorter and he was getting rounder and more out of breath. This year his exercise priority went from a 2 to a 1 with stars and exclamation points around it! Bill decided he was willing to trim his schedule in a few areas to make working out a priority.

For me, writing and speaking are not only my career; they are what I truly enjoy, so they are a high priority. But equally high is time spent forming my children. I love helping with science projects, going to the library, reading aloud to them—so I gave up other things so I can do that. I spend less time socializing with friends; I rarely shop for fun; if I have to choose between cleaning the house and reading to the boys (this is an easy one), I choose the reading.

Rules of Negotiation

Negotiating is dynamite. It can blow out walls and roadblocks that have kept your marriage from the intimacy you've both desired—or it can blow you both apart! It can be a terrific way of connecting with one another and a wonderful precursor to sexual intimacy when you choose your words wisely. But if you become careless with your words or your partner's feelings, then you can tear life-threatening holes in your relationship. Keep these guidelines in mind as you prepare to talk through your goals.

1. Be positive. Most likely, this is not exactly a fun experience for either of you. So remaining hopeful that an agreement and a plan can be achieved is vital. Nothing is ever accomplished by throwing your prioritized cards into the air and saying you give up! At times you may feel a dramatic gesture like that is in order—restrain yourself. Save the dramatic gesture for the confetti you both can toss at the end of the negotiation! Or the romantic dinner or intimate date you've planned ahead of time as a reward for all your hard work.

2. Be verbally aware. Choose words that will open up discussions rather than shut them down. Avoid generalizations like "You always" or "You never." Avoid accusations like "You are so selfish" or "You don't care about what I think." Avoid telling your spouse how he or she feels. Don't tell your spouse that the feeling he or she just expressed is unwarranted. I (Pam) used to try to fix Bill's problems too quickly. Bill needs to think out loud. I'd hear him thinking, overreact, tell him what he should do and expect that that would solve the problem. Wrong! The goal is to try to discover why certain cards have such a value to the other person. Listen to his or her heart instead of reacting to your own fears.

Instead of reacting, I'm learning to say things like "Bill, what do you see as your options?" "How does this make you feel?" "Do you want me to be your sounding board as you list the pros and cons of all the options?"

3. Have a sense of humor. When all else fails—laugh. The atomic bomb isn't dropping here, no one is dying of starvation, the world is not coming to an end. You are simply trying to find a workable plan for your life. That's it. It is important, but if it takes a few go-arounds to come up with one, that's okay. Keep a joke book handy. Or tell a favorite story. Often when I get really depressed over a situation in life that seems hopeless, Bill wraps his arms around me, does a really awful imitation of Sylvester Stallone as Rocky and tells a dumb joke from one of the *Rocky* movies. It is a *really* dumb joke, but it always makes me laugh.

Humor can often help us regain a more balanced perspective. Bill and I collect jokes about marriage, just to keep us laughing at the challenges of life. Here are a few of our favorites:

*   *   *

A couple visited a counselor because they were on the brink of divorce. The counselor asked the wife, "Does your husband beat you up?"

She answered, "No, I beat him up by several hours every morning."

Then the counselor asked the husband, "Do you have a grudge?"

The husband responded, "No, we have a carport."

A little exasperated, the counselor asked the couple, "What grounds do you have for divorce?"

The wife answered, "We have about four acres."

Finally the counselor asked, "Why did you come in here today?"

Together they said, "We can't seem to communicate."

*   *   *

I had a dream the other night that I was approaching the gates of heaven. I noticed there were two gates to choose from. Over the one at the left was a sign that said, "Men who have made their own decisions." Over the one at the right, "Men who have been henpecked." In front of the right gate waited a line of men that stretched as far as I could see! In front of the left gate stood my friend John, all alone.

In amazement I went up to John and said, "This is incredible. There is a huge line of henpecked men, and over here I find you standing all by yourself. Why are you standing here?"

John gave me a quizzical look and said, "I don't know. My wife told me to stand here."

*   *   *

A pastor was standing at the back of the church after service, shaking hands with his congregation. One very sincere lady looked at him admiringly and said, "You are one of the truly great preachers of our day. Thank you for today's message."

The pastor was taken aback by her statement. He mulled it over as he drove home. His wife noticed that he was preoccupied. She asked him, "You seem pensive. What's up?"

He told her about the lady's comment and said, "I was just thinking about how many truly great preachers there are in the world."

His wife looked admiringly into his eyes and said, "One less than you think."

*   *   *

4. Remember, you're fighting for your relationship. During negotiations there is bound to be conflict. Don't panic; slow down and try to proceed calmly. And don't guard your own individual turf. Remember that you are fighting for your relationship. The purpose is not to win your personal Bunker Hill but to take back territory as a team!

In the movie *Apollo 13*, two characters (based on the crew of the real mission) break out in an argument shortly after an electrical short blows a hole in their oxygen tank. The astronauts are living on borrowed time, but instead of working together they argue about whose fault it was. The captain of the ship stops the two crew members in mid-sentence and says, "We're not going to do this."

Just as the astronauts had to work together to return the spacecraft to earth and save their own lives, you'll have to work together to create and save the life you want as a couple. Placing blame doesn't accomplish anything. More often than not, blame should be placed on the stage of life you are in. Most newlyweds are tight on cash. It's a stage; you're just beginning. Parents of toddlers are exhausted from just chasing the kids all day. Most couples in mid-life have intense schedules—work, children and outside responsibilities are at a peak. Parents of teens have emotional battles and busy schedules. That's life. It's not either of you—it's life! Hang the blame on life, and then get on with how you are going to survive and thrive through the stage of life you are in.

5. Keep the conversation going. This may be a process of several steps. The first time Bill and I did this procedure, we had an ongoing argument that lasted nearly a year! Once we sat down with our cards, it was a several-session process because we wanted to look at each area of our life and see what we really wanted out of it. The first time takes the longest; after that, you will simply refine and renegotiate each year as new variables appear.

Even if time runs out and you feel you haven't resolved the problem, commit yourself to affirming your mate. Bill often says things like "I don't have all the answers, but I have you. I love you."

6. Grieve over what has to be given up—then dance on the coffin! Coming up with a workable plan may mean one or, likely, both of you giving up certain personal rights, ambitions or possessions. It's okay to feel sad—for a while. But instead of sulking, plan a celebration. You may even choose to incorporate one of each of the sacrificial lambs you both gave up for "one last hurrah." For example, Bill gave up golf, but I sent him on one last tournament first. At this time in our life, when Bill has a difficult time carving out time for me and the boys, he said he just couldn't justify spending an entire day chasing a little white ball around. So we loaned out his clubs and bought a basketball, because he can have a fun time with the kids and a great workout in an hour, right in our driveway!

I gave up shopping—not shopping for necessities, but the leisurely window shopping of antique malls and gift stores that could easily eat up several hours at a time. Once a year we incorporate a little window shopping into my birthday date.

7. *Write out the new plan.* Put the plan on paper. No one has a perfect memory. In the days ahead you may need to refer to a goal set or a budget worked out. Both of you should keep the plan where you can see it. Bill and I each keep a copy of key goals in our organizers. Then review the plan regularly. Each year, Bill and I sit down and work the plan on a weekend getaway. Sometimes we work the plan each evening for a week and use the getaway to celebrate! Do whatever works.

We review how we're doing quarterly and monthly when we do our calendars. Sometimes, we are forced to review when new opportunities or challenges arise. No one can predict all that the future holds, so you'll have to fine-tune your plan as you go. Fine-tuning is workable since you both know which direction you're headed in!

Love is choosing to hold hands, look ahead, plan, then walk in the same direction.

*   *   *

Time Out of the Tornado
Flashing yellow light! Use this time to write several Post-it notes that say encouraging things about your spouse. Now hide them in the bill basket or in your spouse's briefcase or billfold.

8

TECHNOLOGY

I hate this thing!" Angela said as she threw the pager across the room. "It always goes off at the worst times!"

"Whose is it? Yours or mine?" Jake asked.

"I don't know. I just threw it."

Jake slid out from under the covers and groped in the dark bedroom for the missing pager.

"Here it is. It's yours this time."

"Leave it there and come back to bed."

"Aren't you curious about who it is?"

"Probably some client who's wondering when the paperwork will be finished. It'll wait . . . I hope."

"Just check. It's already ruined the mood."

"Oh, all right. Hand it to me." Angela gazed down at the numbers. They were dim but readable. "It's the office. The office can wait—you can't. Come here!" The pager hit the floor and bounced under the bed. Angela crawled back into Jake's arms with a sense of victory. She'd conquered her connection to the pager.

Then, again, this time from under the bed, came that all-too-familiar beeping. The romantic mood was shattered. *"What now?"*

Technology can be a blessing to a marriage or a distraction that makes your love grow cold. Technology can buy you and your family precious moments, or it can consume your life like an insatiable monster. Your irritations can swell as the answering-machine light beckons you, the pager beeps you, your vacation is spent with a computer on your lap, and your spouse thinks your mobile phone is an extension of your arm. But technology can also keep you connected to each other. Your personal phone allows you to let your spouse know you're going to be late. Voice mail can record those suggestive messages to your wife that let her know you care. And the fax she sends you on your business trip can be just the pick-me-up you need.

Technology can steal your attention because it isn't nearly as demanding as spouses and families. Technology won't force you to confront issues from your past that may be stopping your future. Technology won't complain about your lack of people skills. Technology won't scream, "Please exit program and call up a counselor. You are entering a mid-life crisis."

Technology is here to stay. It has become as much a part of our life as eating and getting dressed. "In fact, whether we approve or not hardly matters. These things will happen. All we can do is try to be prepared," says futuristic writer Connie Willis.[1] William Halal is a bit more optimistic: "Because people are social beings, information services are unlikely to replace direct interaction; rather, these services will offer a viable alternative to the real thing when more convenient."[2]

How can you as a couple manage technology so that it enhances your relationship? How can you integrate technology into your personal life so that it does not steal time and attention from each other? Here are three key principles which will enable you to use technology to enhance your marriage.

Customizing Technology

1. Use technology that matches your style. People live life the way they eat salsa. Some like it hot; some like it mild. Integrating technology is much the same way. Some people like fast-paced, productive, highly interactive lifestyles. Some prefer a quiet, predictable, more private environment. The technology choices you are comfortable with will be determined by how well those choices fit the way you like to live. Explore the options and choose those which fit you best.

Choices must be made in the area of communication. In addition to telephones and cellular phones, videophones will soon be commonplace—that is, if we can figure out a way of blocking the picture when we're right out of the shower, having a bad hair day or still wearing our PJ's at noon. Let's face it, sometimes it is a blessing to be heard and not seen!

Videotelecommunications will give us the ability to see Dad on his business trip, or Mom while she's away, or distant friends and relatives. The rub will come with the need to block the video screen if necessary yet not offend the caller! And how much will show on the screen? Will it bother you if the background display includes your sink of dirty dishes or your desk piled with papers?

Technology is being initiated that may form a personal bulletin board for us. For example, I would like to call Sam Jones. I dial Sam's number and a voice mail system picks up the call. It lists several choices: "Would you like Sam's voice mail to leave a message? Would you like me to contact Sam to see if he is available to receive your call?" I may need to just leave a message with Sam, so I choose voice mail. Or I may need to talk to Sam directly. The voice mail bulletin board will dial Sam, relay who I am and why I need to speak with him. If Sam is available, he can have the machine connect us. Sam may have an electronic screening list, so that a select few are automatically sent through and everyone else gets voice mail. If Sam does want to talk but it is an inconvenient time, he can have the machine relay a better time to call. It's like having a personal secretary at all times.

William Halal predicts a widespread use of a "personal digital assistant." This is a robot computer that can be programmed to handle routine tasks on behalf of its master. This personal assistant will have the ability to gather data and "learn" how you make decisions so, in effect, you could send your PC to a meeting to answer questions. Would you be comfortable with a computer representing you at work? How would you respond if your spouse sent the assistant home to talk through household decisions?

Jaron Lanier, the father of virtual reality, thinks that "in the future we will live part of our lives in cyberspace."[3] But Michael Eisner, CEO of Disney, says "there is no substitute for being there, out there working, traveling, mingling, greeting, meeting, learning . . . pressing the flesh."[4] Nicholas Negroponte, director of Media Laboratory at Massachusetts Institute of Technology, thinks people will learn to balance. "Some people may say, 'TILT! I'm not comfortable with personalized media because I may . . . lose the common threads of conversation. . . . How will I know that Israel just signed a peace accord with the PLO?' You will know, because personalization will not be at the expense of headline events."[5]

Another arena of options is the area of entertainment. The number of entertainment options are staggering. Included in this whirlwind of technology is virtual reality. With virtual reality comes the ability to experience far more than a lifetime could normally hold. You'll be able to travel anywhere and create experiences not available in the real world. You could ride on a dinosaur, for example.

For those who love variety, satellite TV is now an inexpensive reality. For about the same cost as cable, you can now link up to a satellite company that can pipe in over 250 channels! Do you want to decide among 250 channels? How will you ensure that you do not lose society's shared values as you demographically taste only what is pleasing to your TV palate? Couples may find themselves in different rooms now, watching different shows. What will happen when the options number in the thousands?

When you are on-line, your personal life is on display for most anyone with the time or desire to discover it. The information highway is a two-way street. Your finances, correspondence or almost anything else can be accessed—sometimes easily, sometimes by only a trained hacker. "Big Brother" could begin keeping track of what you eat, via the grocery store scanner, and sell that information to your health insurance company. The possibilities are endless. How much do you want to protect your privacy? Are you personally concerned about how much others know about you? You can keep on top of the newest security. You can write Congress. And you can look for ways to personally maintain the level of privacy you desire.

It's very important to protect your time. How plugged in do you want to be? Do you like to receive a lot of messages and keep in touch with current events at work and in your friends' lives, or do you prefer isolation? Do you like to be in the middle of decisions or would you rather be left out of the loop? Recently a friend came home from a week-long vacation to find over one thousand messages on his e-mail. Was he obligated to answer them all? If so, in what time frame?

One corporate president tells of a vacation made possible because of technology. "It used to be a real burden for me to take a week off, but this past summer my family and I rented a place on Long Island. I was able to exercise with the kids in the morning, go to the beach. From 11:00 to 2:30, I had my portable plugged in and I'd return phone calls on my cellular phone. I'd answer e-mail. I'd be in touch with my secretary, who would have updated my calendar online. So I'd work for three and a half concentrated hours."[6] It wasn't the perfect vacation, but at least Dad was along on the trip!

The issue here is that technology forces you to constantly make decisions, so it can appear your life is moving at warp speed. On average, modern Americans have to make decisions on over 8,000 messages per day![7] The pager vibrates. You have to decide if and when to respond. The answering machine records a message. Do you screen the call or pick it up? The faxes, the e-mail, the cell phone—more decisions. Your mind is exhausted each night because you've decided so much. Many are little decisions—but there are so many! How many decisions fit into your style? At what pace do you want to receive information? Seek out the technology that fits your style.

2. *Use technology to say "I love you."* We spent our fifteenth anniver-

sary in Hawaii. After the trip, I (Pam) wanted Bill to have a special lasting memory. I chose a picture of the two of us sunning on a rock near a waterfall. Then I purchased a frame from a high-tech store. The frame was relatively inexpensive and had the capability of recording a message to be played at will. It also held a digital clock. It was hinged so it fit nicely in a desk drawer, pocket or suitcase. I recorded a message full of intimate symbolism that only Bill and I would understand, and I wrapped the gift and placed it in his desk at work with a card. Bill loved the surprise! That was one time when technology was a big plus in helping build our relationship.

Once when Bill was away on a business trip, I sent a fax via the desk at the hotel he was staying at. To protect our privacy, I worded the love note like a business letter, complete with messages full of double entendres. I told Bill I was anxious to work on the projects listed on certain pages of our last book *(Pure Pleasure)!* It's nice to have so many ways to send love notes these days—e-mail, fax, a note on the Internet, voice mail. The future will likely bring even more ways to say "I love you!"

But it will also offer other options. If your real life gets too complicated, or relationships too stressful, you can retreat into a virtual world where you can control all the variables. You have the potential of isolating yourself in an unreal world and losing your real relationships. It might be easier to dial up and interact with an image off interactive TV or CD-ROM than to interact with your mate who is screaming for attention.

You could also surf the Internet and find some virtual sex. Adultery for the next millennium. Advances in virtual reality are making it possible to wear virtual clothes that enable you to sense what you are seeing. It is only a matter of time before high-tech sexual self-stimulation will occur. Instead of real sex with a partner, it will be virtual sex via a machine.

In our book *Pure Pleasure: Making Your Marriage a Great Affair,* we explain that each marriage relationship is unique and should be protected from unwarranted outside influences such as pornography, fantasy literature, other lovers and so on. In a world where sexual stimulation is so readily available via TV, PC or the phone lines, you need to make sure you keep your marriage private and protected so the uniqueness of your relationship can reach its full potential.

The fallout from cybersex will be a sense of personal alienation and overwhelming loneliness. We are social creatures, made to connect on a deep emotional level. It is impossible to produce a cybersubstitute for the emotional, physical and spiritual connection found in marital intercourse.

Another way to say "I love you" with technology is to filter what comes into your home. Are what you're watching on TV, the video games you play, the radio you listen to, the on-line services you subscribe to sending messages that agree with your spiritual and moral frame of reference? By not carefully guarding what comes into your home, you may be planting the seed of decay as you log on.

Trish and Kevin were a little bored in their relationship. They'd been married over ten years and life seemed too intense and responsibilities too heavy—so Kevin suggested they use movies to help them unwind in the evenings after the kids went to bed. At first they'd watch R-rated movies; then Kevin suggested an X-rated sex film "just to give us some ideas." Trish felt uneasy, but she went along. Sex was good that night.

However, Kevin soon wanted to watch an X-rated movie every night. He wanted Trish to try everything on the videos. When she'd refuse, he'd become sullen and withdraw. Trish resented the imaginary lovers' intrusion on their love life. It got to where Kevin would never even approach Trish sexually unless he'd seen a movie first. Finally he stopped approaching Trish altogether.

Trish felt hurt and angry that an image on the screen could rob her of her husband. One day she was emptying the pockets of their suits to take them to the cleaners. In Kevin's jacket pocket she came across an advertisement from an X-rated adult nightclub.

"What's this?" Trish demanded as she threw the ad in Kevin's face.

"Well, you didn't seem to want me anymore," Kevin stammered.

"Me not want you! You didn't want me! You just wanted me to be like those women on the videos! And now this! *Get out!*" Trish stormed away.

Technology had become the first wedge ever to drive Trish and Kevin apart. With the help of professional counseling they decided to purge their life of all trash technology, and they are now working on rebuilding their relationship.

"It's not easy," Trish said. "The trust is broken and has to be rebuilt, and that's going to take a lot of time."

Kevin reported, "I'm sorry I ever suggested the videos. They robbed Trish and me of several years of our life, and I'm still fighting flashbacks. I'm in a men's accountability group, because I know I could easily slip back into pornography, even though it nearly wrecked my marriage and cost me my family."

3. Use technology to create more time for each other. It is wise to invest in technology when it will save time for you and those you love. On one trip, Bill and I met at a desert oasis. Bill was coming from a father-son trip with the boys, and I rode to the rendezvous point with my friend Debbie, whose husband and son were also on the trip. From the meeting point, our family was going on to a wedding and theirs on to a vacation. After we said our goodbyes and shopped for a while, I realized that all my suitcases, including the wedding gift and everyone's wedding clothes, were still in Debbie's car! No problem—we dialed her car phone. She was only fifteen minutes away so she brought it all back to us. That was a disaster averted and hours and hours saved because of a car phone!

Telecommuting and video conferencing are bringing many Americans back home—to work from a home office. Time spent taking the children to the library for that report can be changed to minutes on an on-line service or an encyclopedia on CD-ROM. Calling home on the car phone in traffic can save time spent in needless worry.

The Internet and World Wide Web are growing exponentially, and time spent on the net can easily slip away. What may seem like minutes can in reality be hours. You may be reaching out and touching people around the world through your keyboard—and losing touch with your mate and your children. But before you toss the Internet away, remember, e-mail reaches around the world. You can talk with relatives or missionaries, or with each other when one is away, for a very low cost.

Just make sure you use the time you save for each other! Terry and Jan thought buying a second PC would give them more time together as a couple. It seemed that they were always waiting on one another to use the computer. "I felt like we were in a relay race and the computer was the baton. Terry would do some work, then pass the PC to me. We never spent time together. We wanted to be on the computer at the same time so we'd have more time together after our work was done," Jan explained.

Terry began, "It worked great having two computers—"

"At first," interrupted Jan. "But then Terry wanted to play some computer games to unwind. So I'd surf the Internet and shop on-line."

"Pretty soon we realized that our time apart on the computer was even more than when we passed it back and forth like the baton. Time was just getting away from us."

"We had to get it back under control, set some limits," Jan added.

Terry and Jan are not unique in their PC dilemma. Often families upgrade computer systems until everyone in the family has one. In the future, it will not be uncommon to find every member of the family on a computer at the same time. If Mom and Dad are doing their work while the kids do their homework so everyone can break for dinner and have time together in the evening, families may find it a real time saver to have a PC for every member of the family.

As a couple, you need date time. You need to relax together, talk, debrief and unwind. This kind of casual interaction is nourishing to your relationship. In many marriages, it can become habit to spend time with each other only when a decision needs to be made. Couples become business partners rather than lovers.

You can save valuable time by refusing to give your attention to those who haven't earned the right to take your time. Your spouse earned the right at the marriage altar. Your kids earned the right when they were born. Your mother earned the right when she walked the floor at night with you. Business partners earned the right because they invested time and money in you. It is not a level playing field. Some have earned the right to our time more than others. Your time is a gift you can give to those you love most. You need to protect your time.

Pagers don't have to always be answered, nor do faxes, e-mail, voice mail. Answering machines can be turned off on occasion. It is good to get away to a cabin without TV, radio, phones or laptops! Those we love deserve our time, and somehow we have to manage to give it to them. To protect your unity, set up strict boundaries on the type of usage or the time of usage for your personal computers. Reward your relationship by setting up dates after a specific time on the computer. Romance can get squeezed out in a high-tech world because romance takes time! Time spent thinking of your lover, dreaming of your sweetheart, is necessary for a fulfilling intimate time later. Give your brain time offline to prepare for romance together.

Some people like a mobile phone to finish their day's calls before they hit the door in the evening. Others find this gives them no time to shift gears emotionally before getting home. Before you buy any piece of technology, ask yourself, "How will this bring us together?"

4. Don't get pulled into thinking you have to have everything that is new. Keeping up with the newest technology can skyrocket your techno-budget. Almost as soon as you get the latest and greatest new gizmo home and learn how to use it, it's obsolete. Learning contentment is tricky but crucial. We've seen couples buy the newest and best just as a conversation piece. They are constantly getting new toys to play with—using up all their extra money and their extra time.

Carol and Danny have really been affected by this "got to have it" mania. Danny works in a high-tech industry, so he is drawn to the new and novel. Danny's buying of new technology nearly drove them to divorce.

Danny would just buy and buy. "If it was new, I had to have it, even if I knew we didn't need it: zillions of different radios, including a Harley-shaped one; a pager; electric nose-hair clippers—it became an obsession!

"I was out of control," Danny explained. "We could afford most of it, but I was spending all my free time either buying or playing with technology. I stopped going to my Bible study group. I played with the kids less. And when Carol stopped being interested in my latest gadget, I shut her out too.

"But God got my attention, not through technology but the Bible. One day, in an all-too-infrequent quiet time, I was reading in chapter two of 1 John. Verse 15 said: 'Do not love the world or anything in the world.' Well, I realized my love had shifted. I was loving things more than people. I used to evaluate everything based on how God could use it to help other people. The focus had subtly shifted to how it was going to help me. When I saw it, I didn't like it. Oh, I still keep up on technology, but I don't have to own it all anymore—just what will make my life more effective in helping others."

As we enter the new millennium and live in houses run by computers and controlled by a remote; when we can make ourselves reachable twenty-four hours a day no matter where we are; when we can decide on travel to outer space or a city under the sea as easily as Club Med; then we'll need to be aware that we and only we can protect that which is truly valuable—our love, our relationships, our marriages. Anchor your marriage safe in the harbor of your relationship and steer it out of the eye of the technological hurricane.

* * *

Time Out of the Tornado
Say "I love you" in the traditional way: bring home flowers, light some candles or the fireplace, give a backrub, whisper sweet nothings in your lover's ear, write a poem, dance. Choose one of these options and take a few minutes to say "I love you." Click the mouse on Exit and go have some fun.

Part II
A WHIRLWIND OF OPTIONS

9

THE TRADITIONAL OPTIONS

*I*n *the whirlwind of options* for marriage today, you need to find the one that works best for you. Don't pattern yourself after any one couple in real life or on TV. Read about the options we discuss in the next five chapters; then evaluate and perhaps reshape your own unique relationship.

Ozzie and Harriet may not be living in your neighborhood anymore—or they may! There is a segment of the population that values having all evenings and weekends together. They like the rhythm of a community that has common holidays, common traditions, even common vacations—like summers off. There are a variety of "traditional" life-management options that achieve this Monday-to-Friday work week with evenings and weekends devoted to family and personal life.

Traditional Option #1: One Paycheck
"We really wanted to be around for the kids. We are committed to living on one paycheck as long as possible. It can be done—we're doing it!" says Jessica, a homemaker from California's Central Valley.

"Everyone is convinced that you can't have a home and happy children and do fun things on one paycheck. It is possible! My husband doesn't bring home a huge paycheck. We are definitely only middle-class—but that's okay. We value time with each other, time with the children and time for church and community. If we go without a few things, or wait a little longer for things, or drive only used cars, that's okay—those are secondary issues to us.

"It is tough to buy much less expensive gifts than people give you, but I do make many of my gifts, and that makes them more personal. Because I am free from work outside the home, I can give the gift of time to friends and family. Last year my mom was ill, and I had the opportunity to pick up the slack and do many of the things she usually did. You can't put a price tag on things like that.

"I sometimes feel like a dinosaur—you know, a dying breed of women who believe that life can work when Dad brings home the paycheck and Mom nurtures the family. My neighborhood is pretty quiet during the day. But it's not empty. We have a moms' support group and a kids' play group at our church, and there are many of us there from one paycheck families. We encourage each other.

"We need the encouragement because society really doesn't value what we do. It is so awkward to be asked at a social gathering, 'What do you do?' When I tell people I'm a mom at home, they often say, 'Oh, isn't that nice.' Then they just walk away. People think that I'm not educated or they won't have anything in common with me so they can't carry on a conversation. But I can talk! I'm involved in politics, community issues, school events, and I use my gifts for drama and music at our church. When people get to know me, they find out I have a lot to talk about!"

"The pressure is really on me to encourage Jessica," says her husband, Tyler. "I try to notice what she's done with the house, and I try to tell her nearly daily how much I appreciate her time with the kids. I know she doesn't get much encouragement elsewhere. It is kind of a rough transition after work. I want to come home to peace and quiet. I'm all talked out. Jessica is ready for a break and some adult conversation. We've worked it out. I try to shift gears before I come in the door. It's like a gift I give to Jess."

Jessica adds, "And I try to give him a break to relax and put his feet up after dinner. I also try to save really important conversations until after the kids are in bed. That way Ty can give me his full attention and I don't get my feelings hurt.

"I'm not sure how long we'll be able to live on one paycheck. My parents, and most of their friends, did it their whole life. I want that. I know I needed my mom as much as a teen, or more, than I did as a preschooler. If we can keep swinging it financially, then we'll do it. I've gotten over the status thing. I think women, and men too, are too hung up on what they do instead of who they are. I am comfortable with who I am."

Traditional Option #2: Husband Works Full-time; Wife Works Part-time

"I'm glad Samantha only has to work a little," says Nick. "She enjoys her one or two nights out a week doing demos. And she gets a discount on the products, so that saves us money too. She just feels better having some money to go out with friends or buy a dress or get treats for the kids. She likes spending *her* money when she buys gifts for me. That's a big deal to her. I didn't really mind when my check bought my gifts, but Samantha likes this way better."

Samantha nods in agreement. "I also like it that my check is a buffer. When insurance or taxes are due, there's usually something in the bank. The kids also know it's Mom's money that pays for soccer, dance lessons, vacation and eating out. All that would have to go if we went back to one paycheck.

"I feel like a pretty traditional woman. I spend most all my time focused on the children and the home, but I also enjoy using my gifts and having a short break from the children. I feel like a better mom after I come back. It makes me appreciate them even more."

"My nights with the kids make me appreciate Samantha!" Nick laughs. "It isn't easy handling homework, baths, dishes, story time and whatever emergency comes up that night. It makes me appreciate what Sam does all day."

"That part is really great," she adds. "Nick never asks me what I did all day. And he never complains if the house looks as if a tornado hit it—he's been there. He knows what can happen! Some days are just like that!

"I don't think I'll ever work full-time as long as the kids are home. Part-time is just so nice. It's the best of both worlds. I can be with my children, especially for those big events, and I'm regularly in their classroom. I like the fact that the neighborhood children play here after school. I don't feel like a free babysitter. It breaks my heart that kids so young have to be latchkey kids. If I can make their day a little brighter, that's great. Several children in the apartments nearby come over. They have single moms. Those moms are already stretched to the max. I'm glad I can help. When I try to place myself in their shoes, all the Popsicles and cookies the neighborhood kids eat really fall into perspective. It's a small way to influence my world.

"I want our house to be the teen hangout as the kids grow too. Already my junior higher has his friends in, and I'm glad. I like knowing his friends, and I *really* like knowing what he's doing and what he's talking about. I've thought that I might change jobs when all the kids are in school full-time. I might want a job that matches their schedule more. You know—I'd work five mornings a week or something. Right now sales is fine because it's flexible."

"I don't want it to seem like this works out perfectly all the time," Nick adds. "Sometimes her demos are on nights I have meetings. We have to swap child care with friends or hire a sitter. We try not to do the sitter thing too often, because Samantha never knows how much she's going to make on any given night. Sometimes it barely pays for the sitter!"

"And every week isn't the same," Samantha explains. "Some weeks are promotions and I'm out every night. Those weeks are crazy! Thankfully, there are only a few of those a year."

"I make a pretty good income, but I know life is easier and we live a life that is comparable to our parents' because Samantha works part-time. They only needed one paycheck, but we need that extra half! I think it is too bad the economy is that way. But this option is working for us, so I'm not complaining."

Traditional Option #3: Dual Careers—Nine to Five

"It's a little hectic at times, but it's not too bad. I wish we could make it on less, but housing in our area is outrageous! " Amanda sighs and rolls her eyes. "My parents' house payment is less than a third of ours—and their house is bigger! We thought about moving further out, like to one of the bedroom communities, but the thought of both of us commuting over an hour each way—well, it made us get a headache just thinking about it!

"We have to really keep our outside commitments to a minimum or we'd never have time for each other or the children. As it is, the kids are at the day-care center till 5:30. We usually have an errand or need groceries, or something, so we get home at six. Then one of us makes dinner. We trade off so we each get to see what homework the kids are doing or have done. We chose an aftercare day-care center that had tutoring, dance lessons and scouting. We didn't want our children to miss out on fun kid things because of us. Anyway, their homework is usually done, but we check it and talk about their day and play awhile. After dinner it's already 7:30. We might watch a half-hour of TV as a family, or read together, or get some project done for school. Mostly, we just get everything ready for the next day—clothes, lunches, things like that.

"Sometimes one of us has a meeting. The kids go to bed at eight. I know life will get crazier as they grow and have all kinds of activities during the week and have a later bedtime. I guess we'll cross that bridge when we come to it!

"Saturday is the crazy day. We try to cram all of life into one day. Soccer games, grocery shopping, house cleaning, social events! Last year, I finally broke down and hired a house cleaner and gardener so we'd have more time as a family. I felt like I was turning into Attila the Hun. I was an ogre boss trying to get all the chores done around here. It was ugly. It's a little bit of an expense, but it has been worth it. Some of my friends hire an au pair or a live-in nanny, but I value our privacy too much, I guess, and it's more expensive."

"I agree that hiring help is worth it," said Craig. "Sometimes you have to pay in order to get more time together. We have to be careful not to let that idea go too far though. We could get to where we eat out every night because it's easier. But that isn't normal or healthy. We want our kids to know what a salad fork is!"

Amanda adds, "I took an extended leave after each baby. Then Craig took a leave. That covered the first year of each of the babies' lives. I know not everyone has that kind of family leave policy. We work at really good companies!

"But it was Mom, the kids' grandma, who really made their lives better. She watched them full-time the second year and then in the afternoons when they were in preschool. If I couldn't be there to rock my babies, I'm glad Mom was.

"But that arrangement was tricky too. I had to have lots of talks on how I wanted the children disciplined and cared for. Most of the time she'd readily agree—but once I pushed too far. Mom said, 'If you don't like the way I'm raising the children, then maybe you ought to quit your job and stay home and do it yourself.' That really hurt, but she was right. If I didn't trust her, I did need to stay home. I had to give her space. She did great. I think I was really struggling with my decision more than I realized.

"I probably would have quit, but I went to school so long to get this Ph.D., and I'm working on some amazing breakthroughs in my field. I feel like God called me to science, and I don't want to let him down either. There are so few women, so few Christians in the field. I know I have it good here. My boss lets me off for all parent conferences, for weekly time in the children's classrooms and even a dentist appointment here and there! The morale is good because the company treats people like people. They have an on-site day-care center now, and they offer a range of benefits. For example, I can choose day care or senior care. I can add orthodontia or optical care for a small fee. There's even a workout center—that I rarely use! But I could. But it is still a far cry from meeting our needs as a family. I'm researching flextime so that maybe I could end my day when the kids get out of school. Every step and benefit you ask for takes time, though."

"It's not the perfect life," said Craig. "But it is good. Because both of us work, I have to watch my hours too. I could easily clock in an extra ten to twenty hours a week, but so could Amanda. We have to pace out our career goals. We don't want to climb to the top and realize that we don't even know our children.

"Last year, my dad was very ill. The doctors thought he was going to die. I went to his hospital room. My brothers and sisters were there too. It was really quiet. After we talked to the doctor, my sister and I walked to the cafeteria, and she said, 'I never want this to happen to my kids. Did you notice none of us knew what to say? We don't even know Dad. He was always so busy with work. We don't know him and he doesn't know us.' That was a sobering moment."

Traditional Option #4: Extended Family Living Together

The Waltons was a favorite TV show for many years. John-Boy and his siblings would close each episode by saying good night to one another. Included in the good nights were Grandma and Grandpa, who lived in a bedroom downstairs. By the time the series was over, several children had married, and the grown children lived in the guest house out back. It was the Depression, and extended family stayed together for survival. Some families are still staying together for survival.

"It's hard on us all!" exclaimed JoAnne. JoAnne is a young grandmother, whose boomerang children have returned to the nest with their own families.

"The economy is hard. Our business is floundering, and Renette and Clint just couldn't find jobs. For the sake of the grandchildren, we chose to let them come back home and live with us. But it is not easy!"

"That's for sure," her husband, Tom, agreed. "Sometimes I feel like the kids are so ungrateful, like they expect us to support them in the lifestyle they were accustomed to when they lived at home as teens. Not only can't I—but I won't! They have to take financial responsibility for their lives."

Renette and Clint know that Clint's folks are struggling, but they have their own struggle as well. "It isn't what we planned," said Clint. "We want our own place. We want privacy. Romance is practically nonexistent—and we're newlyweds. We try to give them money to help, maybe not enough, but we want to save so we can get out of their hair!"

"Sometimes I know I take advantage of Mom as a babysitter," Renette confessed. "I don't pay her to watch the kids when I work. I don't want to offend her by offering money, but I also don't want to offend her by not offering.

"I know I don't clean to her standards, so I don't even try. I know it's wrong, and I feel lazy, but I'm not sure what to do about it. If I'm really honest, I feel so insecure about life that I still want to be taken care of too much."

Clint summarized, "We all sit down and try to talk, but it's hard. It sure isn't like Walton Mountain where *we* live! I guess everybody getting along happily is just for TV."

Several generations under one roof is becoming more commonplace, especially in tough economic times and in metropolitan areas where housing costs are outrageous. For the multigenerational household to work, the premium survival skill is the ability to clearly communicate needs, expectations and consequences in a loving yet upfront manner. The host couple, whether it is the older or the younger generation, has to keep the boundaries of the family and the rules of the household in their control. The goal is to encourage productive and healthy living, not to enable irresponsible behaviors. Sometimes those lines get blurry and a third party, like a pastor or a counselor, may need to be called in to moderate an honest and open communication session.

Multigenerational living can work, and it can even be helpful, if it is handled right. Jake and Susan lived with his family while trying to raise a down payment for a house. They approached it carefully.

"We lived with Jake's folks for eighteen months. They wanted to do something to help us save. Since they couldn't just give us the money, they offered to have us live rent-free with them. We made out a contract ahead of time on what financial contributions we would make for utilities, food and things like that. We also made out a responsibility contract, because we wanted to be of help to them while we were there. Jake and I both worked, but I still came home when the kids got out of school. Mom thought it was important to maintain some sort of normal family life for the kids. On the weekends Jake helped his dad remodel the basement. Then we moved downstairs, and it was like our own little apartment. Since we left they have actually been renting it out, and that will help them when they retire.

"I feel close to my mother-in-law. She taught me a lot of things while we lived there. I never would have learned to can food or to wallpaper! I really enjoyed doing those things with her. I know she probably bit her tongue a few times when my kids ran amok. When something really serious did come up, she would always pull Jake and me aside together to discuss her concerns. She would then ask us to get back together with her and Dad after we had talked. I appreciated her candor and her care. And Dad too. He was so encouraging. He'd bring home ice cream when we met a big milestone in the savings plan!

"The children adore their grandparents and are so close to them. I am grateful that our kids have two more people to talk to who share the same values as we do. I've heard horror stories of other families who lived together, but it worked for us."

Traditions come in all styles. In our culture, it was once common for all extended families to live together; later, only the nuclear family lived under one roof. In history, the economic needs dictated the living style. Because emotional and economic needs change, some traditions will evolve into new traditions. Maybe that is where we are in the whirlwind. Our traditions are up in the air. Swirling above our heads. We're just not sure what's going to land and what is going to be carried away on the winds of change.

Survival Skills

If you are going to survive as a traditional couple, these are some skills you'll want to hone:

Goals: Practice setting goals regularly as a team to bring unity.

Growth: If you follow a predictable path because you hate change, it will be easy for a rut to develop. Encourage each other to try new things both as individuals and as a couple.

Simplicity: Keeping your expenses down will help you be able to afford the quieter life that you desire.

Technology: Be open to new technology—but be discerning. For two-career traditional couples, look for ways technology can buy you more time for interacting.

Forgiveness: All couples need to learn how to forgive readily. For the two-career traditional family whose schedule is packed, it is especially important for you to learn to forgive quickly. Your evenings are a premium time to enjoy each other and your family, so learning to forgive will buy you more time together and fewer arguments.

Communication: Traditional couples need consistent, planned time to visit with each other. These couples often have less material possessions than others who are chasing the cutting edge, but they have the opportunity to have more time together as a couple. Learning to express yourself clearly and listen empathetically will go a long way in helping you appreciate the relationship you have. Regular time for communicating may consist of a night out to talk, time around the fireplace, walks in the neighborhood or sitting on the front porch swing.

*   *   *

Time Out of the Tornado

Traditions—every couple has them. Sing "your" song, pull out the wedding album, take a quick trip to your old stomping grounds, call out his or her pet name—right now do something that will remind your spouse of one of your unique traditions.

Time with God
You will want to use some of your time together to develop a strong spiritual bond with each other. Pray together nightly; read a couples' Bible or devotional book; read out loud to each other from books that promote spiritual growth. Promote contentment in your hearts by memorizing such verses as Philippians 4:12: "I have learned the secret of being content in any and every situation, whether well fed or hungry, whether living in plenty or in want."

10

THE SEQUENCING OPTIONS

*P*ulitzer Prize winner Anna Quindlen made front-page headlines when she announced she was quitting her job at *The New York Times* to stay home—to write novels and be with her kids. Quindlen says, "You probably can have it all. Just not all at the same time."[1]

Many women—and men—are choosing this sequencing option. TV anchor Deborah Norville opted for a less stressful evening program after a maternity leave. "This gives me a chance to continue working on my career, but in a venue that will give me more control over my schedule, and let me be less of a guilt-ridden mom."[2] Even the first woman on the Supreme Court, Sandra Day O'Connor, took a few years off the bench to be with her children. She didn't seem to be criticized for choosing the controversial "mommy track."

Unfortunately, the mommy track has received bad press. In a January 1989 article in the *Harvard Business Review*, Felice Schwartz suggested that corporations might benefit from allowing women choices in their climb up the corporate ladder. Feminist writers tried to dissuade Schwartz in their writings by dubbing this choice "the Mommy Track," a term which Schwartz never used but which describes the challenge well. Both mommies and daddies are looking for a workable "track" or system that will integrate their home and work responsibilities. The image for the "parent track" or "sequencing" is a jungle gym rather than a corporate ladder. The climb is still upward, but it has some side steps for the family.

Many women never achieve what their full-time, career-devoted counterparts do. It can be a tradeoff. If Dad takes the parent track, he too may not achieve the results in his career that his work-centered colleagues achieve. However, those who take the parent track do achieve more time for the family. It is an option worth exploring if you are looking for more time.

This is the option most familiar to the Farrel home. We married young, when we were both twenty years old and still had years of education ahead. We each had two years of college completed when we married. After four weeks of getting adjusted, while each working a full-time job, we began the sequencing pattern that has characterized (and looks like it will continue to characterize) our relationship.

First, Pam worked full-time and put Bill through two more years of college. Bill worked part-time. Then Pam continued to work full-time and put Bill through eighteen months of seminary (with a lot of help from our home church). Then we started our family.

Bill worked part-time for a semester and then began a full-time career as a youth pastor while he finished his master of divinity degree. For one year we took a break from schooling; then Pam began a writing course from home and had another son. After our move to San Diego, Bill worked as a pastor while Pam had son number three, then finished her undergraduate degree. We are both out of school at the moment. Bill is planning on pursuing a Ph.D. and Pam a master's degree. One of us has been in school, taking at least one class, during twelve of our sixteen years of marriage.

Because we wanted the boys to have us as primary caregivers, we have chosen to speed up and slow down our education and career goals to better meet their needs. Pam was a full-time career woman and student in the early years, but she slowed her education so Bill could quicken the pace of his studies to graduate. Then Bill worked full-time, juggling his work hours for Pam to return to school on a part-time basis and launch her writing career. Now Bill's work hours and soon-to-be school hours are increasing, so we've both adjusted our home and work responsibilities. Pam will take a break from education for a while. Many times we don't totally give up a personal goal (like schooling) but we cut it to a minimum so the other will be free to grow.

A benefit of sequencing is more time together as a couple (that is, more time than a split-shift parent or two parents working full-time). Also, because we were the primary caregivers, working our careers and schooling around the kids, they received more TLC and training from us directly. I (Pam) have no regrets about the full-time care I gave the boys as preschoolers. I really wanted to be a mom who breast-fed and rocked babies, read books and played with blocks, and had plenty of time to cuddle and explore. I feel very fortunate to have gotten that time.

I also know that boys eat—*a lot!* And our family needs the extra income I can help provide now that they are in school. I also foresee the day that Bill will need much more intense time with them to help them launch into manhood.

The negative aspect of sequencing can be the financial strain. Often, sequencers live off one income at a time when family financial needs are growing, during the early family years. This strain can be lessened by prior planning or by finding creative at-home work options for the partner who is shifting down so the other partner can shift up.

The Smorgasbord
There are many options in this sequencing mode. The partner who downshifts can choose flextime, job sharing, extended leave, part-time employment or work from home. These options still keep the employee in the field yet without the full-time stress and strain.

Others prefer to quit altogether, taking a complete break from school or career. Then, after their children are older, they reenter the job market, sometimes in the same field, other times in a completely different area of interest they have discovered while home.

In the past, this sequencing option was seen as primarily a feminine option. Women typically worked before marriage, maybe into marriage, then quit while their children were home. Women can choose various windows for reentry to the work place: when the last child leaves home, or when the kids are all in junior high or high school, or even when the last one starts school—or, more recently, when they reach preschool age (typically three or four). Each family needs to decide the emotional and relational benefits and liabilities of work. Even part-time work affects lifestyle and priorities at each age and stage of a child's life. And each season of the parents' marriage also has special demands that need to be taken into consideration.

For example, a wife may want to spread her wings a bit at mid-life. Husbands can seem selfish to insist that their wives continue to sacrifice their needs and desires for the sake of the man's career or unrealistic family needs. Women can become resentful or depressed or can experience low self-esteem when they feel their talents and gifts are being endlessly shelved. Full-time paid employment may or may not be the outcome of this mid-life stretch. Time devoted to a wife's concerns in this transition is a wise investment, because it will draw both of you together. If a women doesn't feel a need to fight for her desires, she can often be more clear in her decision-making—and she will still give priority to her husband and children.

In the same way, a husband may need a little extra time for himself and extra TLC from his wife during his mid-life years. He may need to sense his wife's attentiveness and her desire to be with him intimately, and he may long for fun and want her with him. To build your relationship, you may want to adjust your career goals at these vulnerable times.

Other vulnerable times are the children's newborn and preschool years. Those are demanding days, so the parent at home may need some extra time and a break in the evenings. The teen years can be challenging to parents as well; work schedules and dreams may need readjustment stage by stage.

How to Negotiate a Sequencing Move

Here are some steps you can take to formulate a suggested plan and prepare for a negotiating session as a couple.

Lay out the plan for your spouse. Often the sequencing move is more important to you than to your spouse. A husband may feel a need to intensify career goals to achieve an objective, or a wife may see a work-family conflict on the horizon and want to head it off. One parent may notice a special need of a child or desire more time caring for the children. If you have a set of options going into the conversation, that alone may help address some of the common fears. Sequencing can bring up questions like these: "How will we make it financially?" "If I help you reach this dream, what will I have to give up?" "Why is this dream so important—is it more important to you than I am?" "What's wrong with the status quo?"

By seeking to answer the fears that may creep up in your spouse's heart, you'll have a better opportunity to communicate clearly about the issue, rather than having so much discussion based on baggage, peripheral issues and fear-based anxiety.

Find out the details. There are many options available for sequencing a career.

☐ Flextime: This is a popular benefit for companies to offer because it is a low-cost perk for the business. Between 30 and 40 percent of all workers enjoy this benefit.[3] Basically, it is the ability to begin and end your workday as best meets your needs. It can also include the option of a compressed work week, such as four ten-hour days instead of five eight-hour days.

☐ V-time: Voluntary Reduced Time enables employees to reduce their time (and their pay) for a specific period—usually six to twelve months. Workers usually retain their status and benefits on a prorated basis. Companies are open to this option because it avoids the costs (in money and time) of hiring and training new employees. Companies also see this as a way to keep valuable employees.

☐ Part-time: This option portions off days or parts of days for work and leaves larger chunks of time for personal or family concerns. Companies usually do not grant benefits to part-timers, although a few more are offering perks on a prorated basis.

☐ Job-sharing: This option consists of cutting one position into two parts so that two workers share it. Because each of the two needs to pick up where the other left off, and because they may not be at the workplace during the same hours, it requires diligent communication skills and specific detailing of job responsibilities. Benefits are usually split as well. Companies are sometimes open to this option if it is shown that their cost remains the same. It is sometimes difficult to determine individual performance in a job-sharing situation.

☐ Flex-place: This is telecommuting, or working from home using technology. Companies are becoming more open to this option because it can save them money: less office space is needed, and it may help them meet federal carpooling/clean air laws. The disadvantage is that the over-the-water-cooler networking is missed, and supervisors have to adjust to phoning or faxing messages rather than handling communication in person. It is easier to evaluate productivity when performance is based on completing tasks, not just putting in hours. If your hours and output are similar to your performance at the work site, your supervisor should have no reservations about how you are actually spending your time.

☐ Children at work: This option can range from having your infant with you in your office to allowing elementary-school children and teens in after school. Many upper-level managers use this option because they have the authority to create an office that is businesslike and yet meets the need of the child. A more common option is on-site child-care, giving you the ability to spend breaks and lunch hours with your child.

☐ Independent contractor: Your company may be reluctant to keep you on their payroll with full benefits but still need and want your talent and skills. You may consider starting your own business and taking your old employer as one of your new clients. Because of corporate downsizing, more and more firms are outsourcing tasks—even entire departments—that regular employees used to cover. This saves the company the cost of benefits and allows the company to shrink and grow quickly as the market demands. However, you will now need to cover your own benefits and equipment costs. During lean business times, nine out of ten companies will consider flexible staffing options like this.[4]

For your spouse, you'll need to answer questions like: "How much additional expense will there be to implement this change?" "How much less income will be made?" "Where will the budget be cut?" "Who will care for the children?" "How will your new plan affect *my* career?" Fill in as many details as possible.

Talk to your company with a clear, specific plan. Show your boss how your beginning job-sharing, flextime, work from home or an extended leave could benefit the company—or at least not hurt the company. Realize that the company is primarily budget-driven.

Go to the library. Get statistics and examples of companies that have tried and succeeded at what you are proposing.[5] Talk to your professional network contacts. There are probably others doing what you'd like to, or doing something similar. Contact professional organizations. Often these resources are a clearinghouse or at least a reference to point you in the right direction so you can find out the facts you need. Research your company's policies. Consult with the human resource specialist, if your company has one. Identify supportive or empathic managers, then write up your proposal. In the proposal, be sure to include these items.

☐ Salary: If you go part-time, will it be prorated, and if so, by hour or by percentage, or by completing the job? Will your salary remain the same (as in a full-time work-from-home option)? How about stock options, incentives, bonuses?

☐ Benefits: Will these be prorated, and if so, how? Which will be affected—health insurance, social security, retirement? What about sick days, vacation, holiday pay?

☐ Schedule: Detail your plan and try to predict questions like, What if we need you to work overtime in a crunch? or How will we check on your progress?

☐ Duration: How long do you foresee wanting to use this flexible option? One survey showed that the average duration for a flex plan was approximately five years. The range in the survey was from six months to thirteen years.[6] It often works well to offer short increments (or checkpoints) at first to develop confidence in the plan.

☐ Performance: How will it be measured? How will reviews be handled?

☐ Career issues: Will this put a glass ceiling on your chances of promotion? Will it limit you in certain areas such as travel or management? How will you address any negative attitudes of coworkers or managers?

☐ Equipment availability: Who will provide what equipment and resources to get the job done?

Go in with a positive attitude. More and more industries are open to flexible work options. "Flextime is becoming more important to workers who have child-care and elder-care concerns, and we support that," says Beth Ronan, human resources manager for Clark Reid Co., Inc.[7]

Nearly 84 percent of companies already use part-timers; 23 percent have compressed work weeks; 18 percent reported using job-sharing; almost half already have work-from-home options in place, and that number is quickly rising.[8] Almost half of companies who employ part-timers will also provide some form of paid health insurance as a benefit. The most common benefit for part-timers is paid vacation time, followed by a retirement plan option. Companies' attitudes are changing. Business is beginning to realize that part-time employees are as serious about their work responsibilities as full-time employees. It is, in fact, this strong sense of responsibility that drives many couples to look into alternative work options.

Companies are also looking for ways to meet their individual staffing needs. Demographics will shift as the early baby boomers age.

Boomers had fewer children than did their parents, so the qualified labor pool will shrink and companies will look to flexible work options as a way to attract the best employees.

Point out to the management the benefit of keeping you and your expertise "in house" even if it is for fewer hours. Get it in writing! Whatever is agreed upon, write it up and have a superior sign it so that all the details are communicated clearly without misunderstanding. Unfortunately, not all companies keep their family-friendly word, and in the future you might need legal proof of the agreement.

Put the plan on a time line. With your spouse, create a reasonable time line of when and how the change can be implemented for the most benefit. Try to time your proposals in a way that gives the company time but also meets your need.

You might have several options to negotiate. If you want a year off with no pay but the same seniority, ask for it. If the company says no, try for part-time work from home or six to nine months' leave. Keep trying. If the answer is still no, consider other options.

Trust your heart. If you are sensing a need in your family and work needs to flex around the need, God is probably leading you. He may be directing you to another work option or a different life-management option. Stick to your priorities and pray. Seek counsel and trust God for another workable option.

Over and over in our ministry, we have seen parents sensing one of their children needing extra attention. Mothers and fathers have said, "I think I need to work less or find another job that lets me spend more time at home." Usually, it was the intervention the child needed to turn his or her life around. For the few children who didn't respond to this sacrifice of love, the parents have expressed that at least they knew they tried their best, and they did not regret that investment. The parents who didn't respond to the Holy Spirit's tug at the heart usually found the situation worsened. Problems don't go away themselves. Problems left untended escalate into a whirlwind.

Cover your bases. Realize that the best way to make a flexible work option succeed is to try to predict its shortcomings and make provision for those adjustments. If you work from home, your visibility at the office is lessened, so you will want to visit on occasion. If you are using a flexible option to cover a child-care need, plan for emergencies. Have a back up child-care plan available ahead of time in case a client needs you or a problem arises at work. Your company is being flexible for you; try to be flexible for them. Also realize that former full-time coworkers may have a change of attitude toward you. Give them grace. You may be a trailblazer in your company. Your personal skills and gracious attitude may be a key factor in helping others achieve this same benefit, so they can find their own way out of the whirlwind.

Changing Your Mindset

Sometimes sequencing is a change of time schedule; other times it is more a change of mindset. It could be that one of you needs permission to break out of the normal life pattern for a designated amount of time. For example, during my (Pam's) last semester of college, Bill and I were coauthoring a book and I was carrying a nearly full unit load. Bill really freed me from needless worry and guilt by a simple statement, "Pam, do whatever it takes to get out!" We discussed what standards of housework I could drop a level, what items I would take off the calendar—and I got a green light for more prepared dishes and fast food. It definitely took pressure off till graduation in June.

Earlier in our marriage, Bill worked as an architectural draftsman. He was also a student and a youth pastor. We had two tiny boys at home, and life was definitely a whirlwind. One day I was upset at Bill because he seemed so sullen and withdrawn. That evening our conversation hurt my feelings. I went to our room to cry. Then I started to pray. Suddenly God impressed upon me that this night was a turning point and I couldn't let the argument die.

I went out to the living room and saw Bill sitting in a chair studying.

"Bill, this is bad. We're fighting just like average married people, and we don't want an average marriage. What's going on?"

Seeing the distress on my face, Bill put down his book. He reached out and took my hand. He said, "I don't know, Pam. I wish I did, but

I don't know, and it bothers me too."

"You do all the right things, honey. You were there when the baby was born. You call when you're going to be late. You try to play with Brock. You even brought me flowers last week—and you are busier than you've ever been. I really appreciate that you are doing the right things—but it feels like you're not *here*.

"You aren't the Bill I met and fell in love with. You aren't the Bill I've been married to for nine years. When you handed me my flowers, you just held them out with no expression on your face and said, 'Here, I brought you these.' No kiss, no hug, nothing! Lately it's like you are a Bill clone or a robot or something."

"That's it, Pam. That's how I feel. Like a robot. I just function. I don't feel. I'm so stressed over meeting graduation deadlines, work deadlines and ministry stuff that I have nothing left. I'm too tired to feel."

"I can understand that. This is intense. But we can make it—and I can help, if I just know what's going on. I just want you to survive. You're almost there! Graduation is just a few months away. I know the drafting job is paying the school bill so your diploma will be released. I know your heart is in ministry so you're giving the youth group a lot of energy. That's okay with me. I can lower my expectations of you. My C-section didn't take out of me what life's taking out of you! If you'll let me in, I'll help in whatever way I can."

The discussion went on. Bill realized for the first time that his coping mechanism during stressful times was to shut down his emotional center. I gave him permission to do that *if* he communicated that to me. I also made a commitment to lower my expectations to almost nothing, with the promise of a celebration at the end of the stress in a few months. I just needed light at the end of the tunnel.

Now, if either of us senses that we're in one of those "bury your head and run for the goal line" modes, we know we have made a commitment to communicate—to let the other partner know. This way, Bill's emotional atrophy won't wound me and my typical preoccupation and flurry won't wound him. We give space to one another with the commitment of celebrating the goal together at the end. After the celebration, then we regroup for the future.

We have also made a commitment not to live with preoccupation or emotional atrophy as a lifestyle. If the project or job stress seems endless, we confront one another. In love, Bill has told me, "Pam, I feel like your heart and mind are somewhere other than with me and the kids. Is it true or is that just my read?"

A few times it was true, and Bill's loving confrontation helped me refocus and helped us achieve a more workable plan. Other times I've been the one to bring out the calendar and say, "I thought it was just me feeling lonely, but I've been keeping track of your work hours, and the reason I'm missing you is that in the last month you've worked an average of eighty to ninety hours per week. Is this a temporary crisis, or do we need a new plan to get some boundaries back around our life?"

We've always matched schedules so that our time is dovetailed, but checking out intensity levels keeps our hearts dovetailed as well. It is easier to give a little when you understand the heavy weight of responsibility a partner feels or the temporary stress or preoccupation caused by a temporary factor on the job. Temporary sequencing becomes a natural loving response. It is a portrait of unconditional love. Sometimes our partner needs space, encouragement and time to get something off the overfull plate, so that afterward you both can come back and really enjoy time together.

Communicating our sequencing needs can help us avoid unwarranted accusations caused by neglect of a partner. Statements like "You're never here!" "You don't care about me!" "Why are you shutting me out?" are all red flags that signal the need to communicate.

Whether sequencing is used for balance in the long run, during key child-raising years, or in the short run, while you meet professional or educational goals, sequencing must be agreed upon, not imposed. You will never build a marriage by demanding that the other person sacrifice to meet your self-determined needs! But a loving spouse is usually drawn to volunteer or at least be open to sacrifice when you ask for help in getting to a goal.

Survival Skills
If you want to thrive as a sequencing couple, these are the skills you'll want to hone.

Communication: It will be easy to hurt one another's feelings if you demand your right to either slow down or speed up your career. By learning key communication skills you'll be able to clearly explain why you'd like to see the sequencing happen and articulate how it could take place.

Flexibility: Because your roles, job description and family life will be in a constant state of flux, you will both need to flex and adapt in order to honor your established priorities.

Goals: Long-range planning goals are your lifeline. Being able to identify and utilize portable skills in a variety of settings will be to your advantage as well.

Technology: Being technologically savvy will open up more options for your family.

Simplicity: Because your income will rise and fall, and it may sometimes be only the equivalent of one income, you'll do best if you keep bills and physical needs to a minimum. Budget for flexibility. For example, pay cash for large purchases so that long-term debt and monthly payments won't choke your budget but will allow the flexibility you are looking for.

*　　*　　*

Time Out of the Tornado
Halt! Do something right now that will tell your spouse that you really do believe in him or her. Write a card and send it to the workplace; cut out a paper cloud and write "I believe in your dream"; call and say, "I'm proud of you!" Buy some tools (cell phone, briefcase) to help your spouse believe the dream.

Time with God
Waiting your turn requires patience. Develop your trust in God's plan by

posting in a prominent place the Scripture verse found below. Your bathroom mirror, car visor, refrigerator or checkbook are good options. It is necessary to be reminded that it will all work out in God's time.

"Humble yourselves, therefore, under God's mighty hand, that he may lift you up in due time. Cast all your anxiety on him because he cares for you" (1 Pet 5:6-7).

11

THE AGGRESSIVE OPTIONS

*S**helly, down the block,* does it. Mark, two doors over, does it. Karen, across the street, did it for over ten years. I (Pam) do it too. We work from home. A quiet revolution is happening across the country: people are coming home. Home to work, to be with their children, to launch businesses, to escape the crazy commute or to get some control back into their lives. It is estimated by the National Association of Cottage Industries that by the year 2000, more than half of all Americans will work out of their homes.[1] Already, in 1995, 38 percent of all U.S. households contain at least one person generating income from home.[2]

The trend shouldn't surprise anyone. For centuries the home was the place of business. Families worked farms; the home was central to their ability to earn a living. Trades were often carried out from the homes of craftsmen. Today people are grabbing hold of the reins of their lives and taking control back, aggressively.

The benefits from an aggressive option like home-based business are obvious. There are minimal child-care needs, no office rent, no commute. There may be fewer work-related expenses like wardrobe or uniform costs, lunches out and gasoline costs. However, it's not for everyone. You have to be a self-motivator, enjoy isolation or at least tolerate less social contact. You need to be self-disciplined or work can spill over and take over your home. And not every home has the space to house a business.

Link Resources, a marketing and consulting firm, shows survey results indicating that full-time home-based business owners make an average of $58,400 a year compared to $38,300 for people who work outside the home.[3] Not bad for an option that many still picture as a way for a bored housewife to make "fun money"! Much of this quiet revolution has, of course, been made possible by the information superhighway. *Futurist* magazine estimates that by the year 2010, 90 percent of jobs will be "infotech"—that means they are in some way processing or manipulating information. A 1993 U.S. Department of Transportation poll showed that two million people were telecommuters, working at home a minimum of one to two days every week. A 1995 survey showed the numbers rising to 8.4 million full-time telecommuters.[4] The number is expected to rise to 15 million by the year 2000.[5]

According to *Home Office Computing* magazine, most home-based careers are information-based. Business support services (like personnel, accounting and some other previously "in-house" jobs) are now being contracted out to small companies to avoid paying benefits and to make the profit margin bigger during lean times. Desktop publishing, consulting, programming, other computer services, graphics and marketing, financial support services, together with business support services, make up over 75 percent of the home business market. Link Resources estimates 85 percent are white-collar professionals who do most of their work via computer.[6] The information highway may be the yellow brick road leading us back home.

Break Out of the Box

Madeline Swain, an outplacement consultant, encourages the worker of the future to "think outside the box."[7] A majority of these workers of the future seem to be women. One author writing on home-based business estimates that by the year 2000, half of all this country's small businesses will be owned by women.[8] In 1992, women-owned businesses surpassed the Fortune 500 firms in number of people they employed.

Why are women in particular drawn to this quiet revolution? The children! A new generation of women have been told they can have it all—a terrific marriage, terrific kids, a terrific job. Superwoman bought into the "you can have it all" propaganda—but she's realizing that having it all has too high a price tag! The marriage, the kids, the home and her personal life all suffered because she chased the dream of having it all. Home-based business has the components of fulfillment without the price tag of sacrificed relationships. Today's woman is more educated than previous generations. She would like to use her gifts and talents, but she has also realized that her husband, her family and her ministry are as high a priority as her personal fulfillment. She is characterized by her desire for independence, her risk-taking personality and her desire to live life holistically, integrating work, family and social components. She probably has entrepreneurial role models as well (50 percent of all entrepreneurs say they learned to run a business from observing and working with family members).[9] She may also be seeking to own her own business because of age discrimination, if she is an older women just entering the marketplace.

For these same reasons, men have also begun the trek home. The number of men opting for home-based work is climbing. It seems families really want more time together, and they are willing to "think outside the box" and risk a little. Thinking outside the box may not be as hard as you'd think. Fifty percent of all entrepreneurs start businesses in areas in which they have job experience.[10] One researcher thinks entrepreneurs might be nonconformists because they carve out their own path. An entrepreneur is an "innovative person who creates something different with value [added] by devoting time and effort, assuming the . . . financial, psychological and social risks

. . . in an action-oriented perspective . . . and receiving the resulting rewards [and punishments] of monetary personal satisfaction."[11]

Partners in Love and Money

Many couples are creating a combination of marriage and work; they are called co-entrepreneurs. They are linked in love *and* business. The mom-and-pop businesses are returning—this time with a new twist. In prior times, Pop may have been the president and Mom the secretary. Today's couples choose titles like codirectors or cofounders. Or both are given titles that denote their talents, such as VP in charge of sales and VP in charge of manufacturing. Their work hours may vary to meet child-care needs, but they see that as just another valuable asset to their family system. All work is valuable work to these couples. Child-care is written into the job description!

Aaron and Melinda Reinicke are codirectors of a growing counseling practice which was launched seven years ago in San Diego. Aaron says, "I wanted to have more control of my schedule and my working conditions. We wanted to see more direct fruit from our labor." When they began this co-entrepreneurial adventure, Melinda was working as a full-time clinical psychologist for another firm and Aaron was a full-time student adviser at a university with a part-time counseling practice on the side. Aaron introduced the idea of going on their own and beginning a new practice together.

"I was a little apprehensive," Melinda confesses. "I liked the secure benefits of the university. I had to learn to rely more on God than the university to take care of us."

"I laid out a fleece to God," says Aaron. "I told him a figure that I thought we needed to make per month to make the transition. Then I promised the Lord I would give half to him of whatever was above that figure, in addition to our regular tithe. The first month the income was almost the exact figure; the second month it exceeded the figure, and it continued to surpass it for the rest of the year." Aaron kept his pledge. "I was shocked. I attribute the success of our business to God's faithfulness."

"We pray that God will bring clients to us whom we can help and that the practice can continue to meet our financial needs. It is a good faith builder to be on our own," notes Melinda.

Nine associates now make up Reinicke Counseling Associates. But adding staff was a source of conflict for Aaron and Melinda. Aaron wanted to expand, and Melinda wanted to keep it just a partnership. The two continued to discuss the options until they reached a consensus.

Melinda explains, "The timing of the decision came when I was pregnant and cutting back my hours for maternity leave. It was a time of growth, allowing God to impress on me that he loved me just for being his child and not for what I could do for him."

"We were referring lots of new callers out to other therapists because we were booked solid and just didn't have appointment time for them," Aaron adds. "Now we know clients are receiving quality Christian counseling because they're seeing the counselors we personally hired."

Melinda says, "With my boys being small, I've chosen to work only two days a week while Aaron works four days. On the day when we're both at the office, the boys go to their grandparents. On the other day I work, Aaron stays home with the kids. It's his Mr. Mom Day! I'll gradually increase my work hours as they get older. We have wonderful flexibility in our schedules because it is our own business."

All decisions in the Reinicke house and business are made by consensus. "We talk things out. Listen to each other. We don't make a decision until we both feel good about it. We both feel respected. We both have different gifts. We always respect each other's input," notes Aaron. "One of us will come up with the seed of an idea. We bat it around. It ends up different but forever better as it comes out."

The Reinickes have integrated their personal lives and their practice. "Some couples set up a weekly meeting, and I've heard that helps. But we've seen it work for us to just talk about things when they come up."

"Once the kids are in bed, we really do talk. Rare is the day when we don't sit and talk," says Melinda.

"And not just work stuff. Only a small percentage of our talk time is work."

"Aaron often calls home during the day and sings some romantic song into the machine until I hear it and pick it up. We do go out. But I like to be at home—to watch the moon rise over the mountain from our porch. To me the sense of intimacy from talking and praying together can be as fulfilling as sex."

"I don't know if I agree with that!" teases Aaron.

"But we do naturally seek each other out to talk. We have romantic getaways. Sometimes the kids just go to Grandma's and then we come back home and enjoy time alone," explains Melinda.

Working and playing together, like the Reinickes, is positive for many couples because they enjoy each other's company in various settings. But making it work out isn't always easy.

The Good and the Bad

Here are some advantages and disadvantages of working together. Consider your own personalities, temperaments, jobs and current life stages in deciding whether this option is for you.

Positive factors:

☐ Flexible schedule

☐ Freedom to fit work with life stages

☐ Understanding of how the other may be feeling because you share the same business world

☐ A built-in consultant

☐ More control over work

☐ Time with family

☐ Growth together as you work out problems and make decisions

Negative factors:

☐ Partners' disagreement over whether they are each doing their share of work

☐ Administrative nightmare of paperwork and details

☐ Time consumed by management tasks

☐ Potential to be workaholics
☐ Difficulty of finding a realistic pace in work and play
☐ Evening or Saturday work that conflicts with family activity

A Modem for Marriage

Still other people are opting to work for companies but spend a majority of their time at home. One San Diego computer software company recently relocated their rapidly expanding high-tech firm into a very small office. They rented a space just a fraction of the size of their former office complex, with only a reception area, a large meeting room, a storage area and a few cubicles—and they sent nearly everyone in the company home to work! Modems, phones and faxes connect the workers, and everyone is happier. The company's overhead is down, profits are up and company morale is through the roof! Dads are able to make those games and parent-teacher conferences, and moms can pick up and care for their own kids after school.

In many fields, your work hours can be whenever you'd like them to be. Gil Gordon, a pioneer in the field of telecommuting and editor of *Telecommuting Review,* says that telecommuting is a "workstyle that really fits the times." Gordon interviewed Tom Miller, who has been telecommuting since 1985, primarily so he could spend more time with his children. Miller says his telecommuting reduces the stress in their two-income family. "I can tell you one thing, telecommuting keeps me younger."[12]

Telecommuting has its benefits, but because it is a relatively new work option, it still has bugs. For example, if you telecommute for a company, you may be one of the 80 percent who have to fork out the money for all the equipment needed for the telecommuting arrangement.[13] Companies are very receptive to telecommuters because studies have shown an increase in productivity (anywhere from 5 to 100 percent, depending on the survey), but some of that could be workaholism from employees trying to prove the arrangement will benefit the company. Much of the expense for office space and utilities is transferred to the employee—you have to have an office at home, and you are paying for it![14] At the same time, the portion of your home that is used for business is tax-deductible.

Isolation is another common complaint of telecommuters. And not being taken as serious business workers is another. One former CEO, who is now a telecommuting chairman of the board of a high-tech firm, says, "My daughters don't think I'm working unless they see me in a suit."[15]

Married couples who both opt for telecommuting can have the pleasure of seeing each other all day and all night every day. For some couples, that much togetherness is bliss. For others it would be torture! They should definitely not choose this option.

Workaholism is a common complaint among telecommuters. Many telecommute so they can spend more time with family and be the primary child-care providers. This means that they often spend a full day with children, then work until 1 or 2 a.m. For many telecommuters the constant shift from personal life to business leaves them feeling like a ping-pong ball—lots of movement, but they aren't sure what exactly has been accomplished.

As technology advances and becomes more affordable, whole new home office and ergonomic (work and health) ventures will appear to help ease the transition to working from home. Many companies that are familiar with the benefits of telecommuting may also be more willing to pay for some of the home-office costs and equipment, thus opening up the option to more couples.

All Plugged In and Nowhere to Relax

One common complaint among aggressive couples is that work can become all-consuming. The paperwork creeps out of the home office. Its subtle tentacles wind around coffee tables; they can even silently stretch into the bedroom. The phone calls can be unceasing—sometimes not even taking a break during the night! Dinner conversations can easily drift into the business arena, until the kids one day ask for a vote or a chair on the board of directors. Families and couples that once played together can find it impossible or unnatural to relax. The whirlwind seems to enter as a stealth enemy of romance. Often neither partner sees it coming until someone makes a horrible mistake—like asking a business question in the middle of sex!

Because these are usually type A, gung-ho, get-the-job-done, no-nonsense, assertive, high-energy individuals, their only hope of maintaining balance is to turn some of that energy toward the home front. Assign a person to watch boundary violations. Have one partner watch over work hours. Be co-referees, and penalize the partner who dares to talk shop over the pot roast. (Offsides: the penalty will be one backrub!) Keep a sense of humor. Create a personal incentive plan that rewards nonentrepreneurial effort used in building the relationship.

Personal Perk Plan

If you and your spouse are working too hard at home, choose a few of these ten perks and enjoy them to the fullest. You will still get plenty of work hours in.

1. Have breakfast out. Talk shop for the first half, but after breakfast stop by an antique store or go for a walk on the beach or in a park.

2. Go for coffee. There are lots of relaxing little coffee houses to catch a few quiet minutes together over coffee, herbal tea or ice cream.

3. Exercise together or relax in a spa.

4. Plan an extra day or two before or after a work conference. Spend it relaxing together.

5. Celebrate at the end of a project! (Create deadlines or goal markers if you have to. Find something to celebrate as a couple.)

6. Have an intimate rendezvous during the day. (You do work from home; you can close the office for an hour—you're the bosses!) Give new meaning to that answering machine message, "We can't come to the phone right now . . ."

7. Send flowers home—or call up a loyal client and ask if you may send flowers to your spouse at a meeting in their office. (Half the fun of getting flowers is getting to brag about your thoughtful spouse!)

8. Have personal contact. Touch one another. Hold hands while discussing a decision. Kiss when you leave and return. Give a passing squeeze or pat. Since you're the bosses, you set the rules! Enjoy the privacy of working at home.

9. Take turns debriefing and destressing one another. Make it part of your job description to plan regular dates and relaxing procedures to help each other shift gears.

10. Pray together. Ask God for the ability to maintain a healthy integration of work and marriage. (After all, God started this coworker relationship with Adam and Eve!)

Survival Skills
And keep working at your ongoing skills.

Communication: You'll be talking a lot on the go, so good communication skills are a must. You'll be negotiating in all areas of life. Children, business and personal issues will be intermingled. Learn to listen effectively, and use those skills to help you shift emotional gears quickly.

Goals: Understanding both linear and portable goals will be important because no one else will set the agenda for your life.

Coordinating: You will need to integrate your lives regularly. Regrouping and flexibility are premium skills for those living on the cutting edge.

Technology: Keeping abreast of changes in technology could add profit to your business, thus benefiting your family. Technology can also open up new fields for the home-based business.

Forgiveness: Since you can't leave your business partner at the office, you'll need to forgive quickly and thoroughly. Bitterness and unresolved conflict are time and energy drains, and your time is already short, so prompt forgiveness will buy you extra time together.

Simplifying: Your life is more complex because you balance so many responsibilities. Deciding which peripheral responsibilities you can shed will give you greater ability to shift as market needs arise and as personal priorities need to be addressed.

Growth: You two will have ample opportunity to grow as a couple and as individuals, so your task will be to pace the rate of growth so that you'll stay connected and not grow apart. Each of you will need to share verbally all the exciting opportunities and challenges you see. It's easy to become focused on your own area of responsibility, and you may be tempted to run your decision-making as you did when you were single. Remember you're a team now.

*   *   *

Time Out of the Tornado

Communicate! Tell your spouse what you'd like for your birthday or Christmas. Give him or her a list of favorite dating spots and favorite movies. Tell him or her what sexual nuance that he or she does that really pleases you. Ask your spouse to share the same information with you. *Just say it!*

Time with God

Unity is essential to your marriage's success. Being in tune with God will make it easier to be in tune with each other. Begin each business day together with prayer. Proverbs 16:9 (NRSV) is a good reminder: "The human mind plans the way, but the LORD directs the steps."

12

THE STRENUOUS OPTIONS

*T*om *checks and rechecks* his watch as he sits in bumper-to-bumper traffic! *Not again! Carol is going to be crazy! Maybe I can take Fourth Street and get home faster. At least she'll only be ten minutes late for work.*

"Where is he?" Carol paces back and forth. She tries playing with the baby to distract her mind from the ticking of the clock. "I guess I should call in. Let them I know I'm going to be late again."

"Hey, I'm here! Sorry! Go. Go. Go!"

Carol grabs her keys, kisses Tom and the baby and spins out the door like a cyclone. Day in and day out, Tom and Carol repeat this whirlwind of a schedule. They are part of the growing number of couples that seek to meet their family's child-care needs with tag-team parenting.

The Split-Shift Whirlwind
The typical split-shift schedule has Mom at home for eight hours, then Dad comes home to parent so Mom can go to work. This is the pattern chosen by families who feel the need for two full-time incomes but

prefer to do their own child-care within the family. (They may not have the finances for licensed child-care, and their extended family may live too far away to assist.)

Tom works full-time for an engineering firm. He has a predictable 7 a.m. to 4 p.m. work schedule. Four nights a week and on Saturday, Carol is a hospitality coordinator for a large hotel firm. Carol cares for the children while Tom works, and then Tom relieves Carol so she too can pursue her career.

"I like to get out. And this is a good way to use my talent and make a financial contribution to the family," says Carol.

"I like the intense 'dad time' it gives me." says Tom. "I think I have a better understanding of what Carol goes through being mom to four kids under five! Some men wouldn't understand the hard work their wives do. But I do! I truly appreciate Carol. It really makes me love her more!"

Carol adds, "We know this is only temporary until all our kids are in school. As it is now, we are pretty tired all the time, and we really miss each other. I value the time we do have, and I'd like even more time together."

"Most of the problems that split-shift workers experience occur when their family responsibilities collide with the need for sleep," says Marty Lien, president of SynchroTech, a management consulting firm in Lincoln, Nebraska. "Parents will cope with a great deal of fatigue in order to live up to their obligations."[1]

How can you survive the split-shift whirlwind? Here are three suggestions.

1. Make specific time to communicate. You may need to rely on notes or phone calls back and forth from the job site. But you need at least a few minutes daily to be face to face and communicate your love as well as the details of life!

2. Carve out time as a couple. Your living style gives you very little time together. It will be easy to create two separate lives if you aren't careful. Couples who never see each other have a difficult time staying in love. The romantic fires need to be stoked on a regular basis.

Maintaining a standing weekly date can be the light at the end of the tunnel that can get you through.

3. If possible, make this a temporary lifestyle. Many couples see the split-shift as so demanding that either lack of sleep or lack of intimacy will cause them to negotiate a different arrangement as soon as possible. Your split-shift can be just the thing, short-term, to help you get one spouse through school or keep the kids out of preschool. But it is the rare couple that can sustain both this schedule and an intimate relationship year after year.

The Commuter Couple Whirlwind

It is estimated that nearly one million couples in the U.S. commute not to their jobs but to their marriages.

A large majority of those couples do not have children. Comments on commuter arrangements range from "It's like a minivacation every few weeks" to "You can't compare two days a month with being there every day." Maura Manning Comford, a design director for Ralph Lauren, says, "Don't let anyone tell you living in two places is easy!"[2]

Gail and Paul found themselves in a commuter marriage when Paul's construction firm couldn't find any local work. For three years he had to travel to different states to oversee jobs. Gail was a teacher. They didn't know what the economy or the construction industry was going to do, so they didn't want to relocate only to have construction dry up in the new location too.

"We treated those years like our early dating days. Each time we were together, we'd plan the next time we'd be together. The phone bills were outrageous. We used e-mail and faxes a lot too! And we Fed-Exed more during that time than we ever have since!" laughed Gail.

She continued, "Some of the construction sites were great—like Cancun, Mexico and South Florida. Others were a real drag, like the cheese factory built in the middle of the desert! Sometimes I would get to go with Paul. Those were like second honeymoons. Sometimes, though, we'd have big fights, because I'd have to make decisions apart from Paul when he was so far away and so busy. We had to work at communicating. We had to get specific about what kinds of decisions I could make independently and which needed a phone call or face-to-face discussion.

"I have a friend, Jill, who is married to a fireman, and she lives like this all the time. The friendship with Jill helped me realize I was making some decisions just to get the upper hand or for power. And Jill's husband helped Paul to see that there were a lot of decisions he just needed to trust me on."

"The trips back and forth were the only joy I had during many of those months," explained Paul. "It was so great to see the kids. I missed so much of their lives. They knew I had to do it to provide for the family, but it was still hard—and lonely. I can see how guys get into drinking or other women. The loneliness is so devastating. I'm really thankful that an older man in my church took me aside at the beginning of this thing and explained to me how he handled his traveling sales job and the stress of being away from the family. I asked him to hold me accountable for my faithfulness to Gail. He called my cell phone once a week to see how I was doing and to encourage me. It was and is a great relationship. I also learned to plug into a local church quickly. I went to Wednesday-night Bible studies and home fellowships with a lot of strangers during those months— but I also made a lot of new friends across the country."

Here are three suggestions for surviving the commuter whirlwind.

1. See it as temporary. There are only a few couples who can live two separate lives in two separate cities and not end up divorced. Try to picture your life together as one life with two extensions, and work to communicate on everything!

2. Weigh the financial costs against the financial benefits. Then purchase the ability to communicate and see each other as much as possible. Look into frequent flier miles, e-mail, a fax machine, pagers, cell phones, an international personal 800 number—whatever will help you communicate often and regularly. Plane tickets are still cheaper than a divorce.

3. Make the times you are together memorable. You will need face-

to-face time to work out the details of life, but try to get most of the chores and errands done while you're apart so they won't eat up your time together. And try to arrange a long enough time with both of you at home, when it finally comes, so that you can celebrate and enjoy each other romantically. Have fun as a family! Realize that both of you may have to give a little in your career in order to get this time.

Strenuous times are not all bad. It is during the difficult circumstances of life that we find out just how strong we are. We try new things, we find new character and we discover new potential. It is often during these times that we find out what a relationship with God is all about!

Your spouse may not be available, but God is always there. Your needs may not be met to your comfort level, but God can bring inner peace that goes beyond circumstances. Life may become the challenge that teaches you just how big God is. "God is our refuge and strength, an ever-present help in trouble" (Ps 46:1). God can give you the strength to make it through.

Make it your goal to be remembered as tough people, not just people who went through tough times.

Survival Skills

If you two are going to survive and thrive with your limited time together, then you'll want to hone these skills.

Communication: You'll have to talk about a lot of issues in a very short amount of time. Your communication needs to be strong and refined so that you can get below the surface quickly. You'll also need to be able to communicate specifically and maintain a hold on your emotions. You don't want to spend your precious time arguing just because of a mismanaged tongue.

Simplicity: The time you have together is precious. Schedule these times as regularly as possible; highlight them on your calendars. Simplify these times by shutting off phones, pagers, faxes and other distractions that can cause you to neglect each other while you are together.

Forgiveness: Because you two live on borrowed time, you'll need to be able to forgive each other quickly, almost instantaneously. Harboring bitterness and anger is actually easier for you, because you can hide your feelings for the few hours you are together. Because you aren't forced to reveal your real emotions, you may be tempted to stuff them until you explode.

Technology: If you find yourself in a strenuous marriage option, you will need all the advantages of technology. You may need to take advantage of many long-distance communication devices.

Relationship: You will need the perspective that says, "We are more important than anything in this situation." You may need to regroup and redefine often, even if it's by phone or letter.

Goals: You'll need to become adept at discerning portable skills, so that if an opportunity arises that can free up more time for you two, you can take it. There is a path out of the hurricane, but it may take some creativity to find it!

Coordinating: You two will need a day-by-day game plan. Flexibility and a desire to weave all the needs of the family into one plan will gain you sanity during an insane time.

* * *

Time Out of the Tornado

Write a terrific love note! In twenty-five words or less, tell your mate how your heart, soul and body long to be with him or her. Try lines like, "In your arms, babe . . . just a few hours and I'll be there!" or "You, me, together, later!"

Time with God

Each of you will be greatly helped by choosing a trusted friend whom you can call anytime, who will pray with and for you during stressful times. Always choose a friend of your same gender, so that unexpected emotional attachments will not start. Remind yourself that God has a plan for you even when life seems out of control. You might like to memorize this verse:

" 'For I know the plans I have for you,' declares the LORD, 'plans to prosper you and not to harm you, plans to give you hope and a future' " (Jer 29:11).

13

THE UNEXPECTED OPTIONS

*T*ravis whistled while he riveted in his final bolts. *Just a few more minutes and I can meet Kelly and the kids at the park for ball practice.* A sudden jerk shook him out of his daydream. He felt the scaffolding creak and lurch. He looked down. Below him, three stories down, were the daggerlike rebar ends sticking up from the cement floor like stalagmites. The scaffolding creaked once more; then he felt himself plummeting to the ground.

"This is going to be bad. Help, God!" Then everything went black.

Travis awoke in the hospital to the faces of emergency technicians and doctors trying to save his life.

"It feels like a sharp knife in my back. Did one of those rebar ends stab me?"

"Luckily, no, you fell between them," said a masked face above him. "Mr. Jacobson, you have a very bad back injury. We think you'll walk again. We're doing everything possible."

Suddenly the lights above him began spinning in circles. He felt sick to his stomach, yet unable to move or speak. He shut his eyes and hoped it was all a bad dream.

"Mr. Jacobson. Good news. You should be able to walk. In fact, we'd like to see you try today. But your back has suffered extensive trauma and you will never be able to work in the construction field again or do any other manual labor."

Sometimes, in a moment's time, life turns upside down. The perfect life, the one you have planned down to the detail, is gone. You try denial. You may bargain with God. You may be angry or frustrated, but none of those feelings change the circumstances that altered the course of your life. When plan A isn't an option—then what? How can you hold a marriage together when life's circumstances are pulling you apart?

Live in Hope, Not Denial

Kelly said, "When Travis fell, I was in denial. The doctors talked about surgery, so I thought it would be the magic cure. Surgery would be the answer to our problem. I saw the fall as a temporary setback. Travis would be back to normal in a few months, and we could go on with life. I really wanted it to be the answer. We had three kids, two in preschool. And I was only a part-time preschool teacher. You can't live on that!

"Travis had a series of operations. It was two years later when the reality of it all hit. By then I had a full-time job; Travis had just had another operation. I was pregnant with our fourth, and it was almost Christmas. I thought we'd have a cozy little holiday. I figured things would be tight but we'd soon be over this obstacle holding back our lives."

"That's when we got the news that my surgery had failed."

"The news was devastating."

"But not as devastating as almost losing you," Travis added with tears in his eyes. "That same week, Kelly lost the baby, and she really bled. The doctors thought they were losing her. I was scared! Really scared!" said Travis. "But she came through."

"But I wasn't coping well," Kelly explained. "I was constantly fighting depression. I had supportive family and friends but still felt isolated. No one could change what was going on. It was compounded disappointment."

"I was fighting it too," Travis explained. "When the surgery didn't work, I felt something must be wrong with me as a person."

"But something happened in our hearts. We didn't have any money. Our family and our church brought over gifts and food. We were overwhelmed with the love. A tiny crack of hope came through. It wasn't denial—thinking we'd wake up and everything would be back the way it was before. It was hope—hope that we'd somehow get through it." Kelly smiled as the memories rolled out.

"I rededicated my life to Christ. I knew God loved me and my family and somehow he would work it out. That was a new feeling for me," Travis added.

Kelly smiled. "That was one of our favorite Christmas memories. We recommitted ourselves to each other and to our marriage. There was renewal there under our little tree lights. It was a new beginning. Instead of focusing on what we didn't have, we began to focus on what we did have. We had each other."

Live in Today, Not Tomorrow
But Travis had to have another series of surgeries.

Kelly continued, "And then the court battles began. No one wanted to cover his disability. We had several insurance policies, and they all denied their responsibility for coverage. Money was even tighter! And the frustration was compounded by the inhumane treatment by those in the system."

"I really credit Kelly. She hung in there. She loved me. Not for what I could or couldn't do—just for me."

"I knew I had to live today," she said. "I could keep hoping for tomorrow, but I had to live today. For me, a lot of strength came in the investment I'd already put into the relationship. It's a tenacity that says, 'Nothing is going to separate us!' It is stubborn love. Seeing the best in the person and not letting the lies of Satan get a foothold in your heart and mind.

"We had to clearly communicate our expectations, then work with those expectations," Kelly continued. "We had to live even in the bad circumstances. We wanted to build, not tear down, during this tough time—even though we had no idea how long it was going to last. You have to make the best of the circumstances. Either make the best of it or it will destroy you. It is a decision. A choice."

Live in the New Role
"By far the toughest factor in the accident and disability was the role reversal that was forced upon us," Kelly noted.

"I was used to hard physical labor," said Travis. "I used to be able to see the fruit of my labor. I built things! I could point to something and say, 'I helped create that!' People valued my work. All of a sudden I was home, learning how to baby-sit. I really feel for moms at home. Society doesn't value their work. And the work doesn't stay done!"

"At first the role reversal was scary," Kelly added. "But then I saw it could be a chance to develop myself and my talents. In some ways it has been good, because I've developed talents I'm not sure I would have used otherwise. But the excitement of the growing process wears off."

"I loved being home with the kids," Travis beamed. "I felt that was my one positive contribution. Right after each surgery, I couldn't do much. That was hard on me. The more I can do for the family, the better I feel. I liked the field trips and time with the new baby."

"But I missed the kids. I was gone all day; I couldn't see them till dinner time. I had to find a new way to relate with them," said Kelly.

"And I often laugh because now my friends call Travis for his recipes! Seriously, to other couples going through this, I'd say, 'Keep things in perspective. The danger in role reversal and this kind of family trauma is that you two can grow apart. Women who feel pushed out of the home can get caught up in a career. You can easily create two separate lives under the same roof. You have to be really, really supportive of one another, whatever the contribution of each one is.' "

"Get people around you who are *for* you and your relationship," adds Travis. "They'll cheer you on when it's rough. And be humble. Accept and be grateful for what your wife or others do for you."

"Be willing to fight for your relationship," Kelly boldly interjected. "Fight for each other and with each other—that's hard to say, but the thing that hurts the most is sidestepping issues. I had to learn it was okay to disagree, and I had to learn to keep a discussion going instead of pouting or clamming up, because until we talk it out we won't get it resolved.

"Sometimes you need outside intervention when the tough times hit. Counseling really helped us. We sought professional help with a counselor and our pastor, and we also spent a lot of time with couples who'd made it through rough circumstances."

Live in Reality, Not in Regret

Saying "If only . . ." or "Why . . ." will drain hope from your marriage. Blaming or silently resenting will build a wall between you. Fighting for rights or guarding power or territory will divide your efforts.

"We had a head start," said Kelly. "We didn't see the money as *his* money or *her* money. It was always *our* money, no matter where it came from.

"If I could give any advice to couples in unexpected circumstances, I'd say build a spiritual life together. Travis and I have taught a home Bible study together for many years. Being in the Bible weekly, preparing for the group, was a great way to keep the right perspective on life. Being in ministry helps you keep your perspective outward. Helping other people makes your problems seem less intense. We also keep journals. I keep a log of prayer requests and how God answers. All this has helped us have compassion. Our kids didn't have everything, but then, they didn't need everything! They have gotten to do some wonderful things with their school and ministry and travel. God always provided. God has done amazing things even in our circumstances.

"We're thinking about renewing our vows. We really are two different people from the ones who got married nearly twenty years ago.

We've fallen in love all over again."

Whirlwinds of Change

Sometimes the death of a child, the illness of a family member, the job of caring for an elderly parent or some other unexpected crisis throws your marriage into a whirlwind. Sometimes a job loss will cause an unexpected role reversal. You are not alone if your "traditional" roles are switched. The U.S. Census Bureau estimates that there are nearly three million kids being raised in a home where Dad is the primary caregiver. The number keeps rising year after year. There are even newsletters and organizations for the "Mr. Moms."[1] This option is strenuous only if it was forced upon you unexpectedly or if one or both of you are uncomfortable with the role. This whirlwind can actually turn into a wonderful blessing for a family, depending on how it is handled.

Here are some hints for surviving the crisis whirlwind.

1. Realize that you each grieve differently. Grief will hit your life when crisis brings loss. Give each other space to grieve. Different things will set off the sadness in each of your hearts. Let it be okay to grieve differently.

2. Don't grieve alone. Create times to talk with each other. Also seek to build a support network of others who are sympathetic to your situation and supportive of you.

3. Carve out niches of "normal" time. Many hours are being gobbled up by the crisis—and most of your emotional energy as well. It may feel strange, but try to find a way to do the things you loved to do before the crisis.

Go out on dates. Walk in those old familiar special places. Listen to "your song." Life won't always be so sad, so demanding and so strenuous. Do whatever it takes to protect that special bond you have as a couple. One couple who were caring night and day for their high-risk infant asked their family, friends and church to pitch in to hire a highly trained nurse to care for the child for a few hours a month so they could escape and do something "normal" as a couple. This normal time may be what keeps you together.

4. Try being teammates. Communicate new role expectations clearly and without hurtful words. You are trailblazing, so think of it as an adventure. Even if the initial reason for the role reversal was out of your control, your response isn't out of your control. Think creatively. Find your own family path.

Survival Skills

If you two are going to survive and thrive in a world that has turned upside down on you, then you'll want to hone these skills.

Communication: You'll have to talk about some pretty touchy subjects, like role reversal, sexuality, loss of income, self-esteem and so on. Your communication needs to be strong and refined so that you can get below the surface level. You can't sweep things under the rug—your circumstances will demand that you deal with issues as they arise.

Simplicity: You will be at a great advantage when a storm hits if your living expenses are low. If they aren't now, consider how to simplify or sell off assets to buy you more time together and more time to decide any future goals.

Forgiveness: You will both have to be able to identify your misconceptions and anger toward God for the storm that is in your life. The Bible clearly teaches that God is incapable of evil and his desire toward you is always for your best interest—but it doesn't always feel that way. You'll need to adjust the six statements of forgiveness to release any bitterness you feel toward God. It's easy to blame yourself or each other for the tragedy; avoid that pitfall. Walking through the statements of forgiveness often will help keep your focus on solutions rather than irritations.

Technology: If you find yourself in a unexpected whirlwind, use technology to call for help. Get on the Internet; post messages on electronic bulletin boards to see if you can find other families who are experiencing similar difficulties. Make it your goal to encourage others, and you will be encouraged in return. If your situation involves a chronic condition that forces a change in the type of work you do, you will want to explore how various technological advances can provide new career options.

Relationship: Your marriage is of top importance! It demands that you fight for your relationship. Tell yourself and your spouse over and over, as often as you can, "Together we'll get through this."

Goals: You'll need to become adept at discerning portable skills you possess. You will need to tap into all your organizational, relational and coping abilities to handle the ups and downs that life is throwing at you. Ask each other, "What are we good at that can help get us through this?" Consider asking trusted friends to answer that question about you.

Coordinating: You two will need a day-by-day game plan. Weaving all the needs of the family into one organized plan (and then staying flexible) will make life seem more "normal" and will provide stability and hope.

* * *

Time Out of the Tornado

Crash! Collapse! Breathe a heavy sigh. The crisis tornado can be exhausting and depressing. So bring some cheer—learn a joke to tell your mate, bring home squirt guns for a water fight, buy and perfect a stupid magic trick—the sillier the better! Try to remember to laugh—tornadoes seem quieter when the laughter is louder.

Time with God

Your hope will be challenged often as you make the necessary transitions in your life. Remind yourself of the steadiness of God's love by decorating your home with reminders. Look for Bible verses that are of great help to you personally; post them in prominent places. Some of our favorites are these:

"We were under great pressure, far beyond our ability to endure, so that we despaired even of life. Indeed, in our hearts we felt the sentence of death. But this happened that we might not rely on ourselves but on God, who raises the dead. He has delivered us from such a deadly peril, and he will deliver us. On him we have set our hope that he will continue to deliver us" (2 Cor 1:8-10).

"We also rejoice in our sufferings, because we know that suffering produces perseverance; perseverance, character; and character, hope. And hope does not disappoint us, because God has poured out his love into our hearts by the Holy Spirit, whom he has given us" (Rom 5:3-5).

"But as for me, I will always have hope; I will praise you more and more. My mouth will tell of your righteousness, of your salvation all day long, though I know not its measure" (Ps 71:14-15).

"There is surely a future hope for you, and your hope will not be cut off" (Prov 23:18).

14

PROTECTING YOUR RELATIONSHIP WITH TRUST

*I*n 1947, a Pan Am plane took off from Cuba to Miami. Inadvertently, the plane caught up with the hurricane that they were supposed to follow. The plane flew into the eye of the storm! Seven of the passengers fainted from fright. The plane was tossed straight up one thousand feet, then dropped just as far. The lightning was blinding. A ball of fire leaped across the wing. Rain fell in sheets so hard that passengers could no longer see the engines on the wings. Rain flooded into the cockpit. Hail beat down so hard that it sounded as if the wings were being ripped off. The frightened passengers had no choice but to trust the flight crew. The flight crew had no choice but to trust their instruments. The plane circled Miami for an hour and a half looking for an opportunity to land, but the airport remained closed because of dangerous weather.

The crew was directed to fly north. With the help of air traffic controllers and accurate flight instruments they finally landed in Nassau. When they touched down, the crew was given a standing ovation.

Trust Is the Key

The individuals on that plane flight survived because the pilot trusted the instruments. In the desperation of the crisis, the passengers were intensely aware that the only possibility of survival was to trust the crew—who was trusting the instruments. Trust in the face of immense crisis is what was applauded when the plane finally landed safely.

In our marriages, trust is the glue that holds a relationship together when the whirlwinds of life seek to tear it apart. The key to effective communication is trust. The key to financial cooperation is trust. The key to sexual fulfillment is trust. The key to progressive decision-making is trust. The key to life as a married couple is trust.

Mel and Vyonda Benson have been married for over fifty years and have been able to keep the love in their marriage vibrant. They have done this despite significant obstacles. Early in life, Mel was diagnosed with rheumatoid arthritis and San Joaquin Valley Fever. As a result, he was forced into early retirement, making just one-third of his former income.

They had to come up with a new plan to meet the needs of the family. For a time they cared for elderly boarders in their home. They planted a garden and raised livestock. Later they built rental units. Their plans shifted, but their love and trust in each other never wavered.

Their now-grown daughter summed up their life: "We didn't worry. We knew Mom and Dad would make it. We knew they loved each other, so there was a lot of security."

Mel says, "It's genuine love. As years roll by and you help each other, work together and cooperate, that builds love and respect."

Vyonda echoes this same practical approach to trust: "We worked together. If something came up and it needed done, we'd do it! We knew we had to stick together. We had to communicate. We had to talk things out. We trusted in God and we'd make do."

We often get sidetracked because we think trust is an emotional feeling. It is actually a choice of the will. Trust is not a haven your spouse gives you but rather a position of courage you develop as a personal responsibility. Trust is not a condition you find yourself in as a couple. It is a characteristic you must develop within yourself first and then invest in your marriage. To put it simply, only trusting people can build trust in marriage. Trust is a muscle that grows stronger with use. The more you trust, the easier it becomes to trust.

Verbalize Your Spiritual Growth

So what skills must a couple master in order to build trust? The first skill is to *share with your spouse the progress you are making in your personal spiritual development*. Some couples find this to be quite natural, but most confess that it is a struggle. John and Nancy discovered the value of sharing their spiritual development, but they discovered it in an awkward way.

"Nancy, I know what's wrong with you! You are believing lies about who you are, and it's causing you to be insecure and self-defeating." John shared this "good news" with his wife with an air of triumph in his voice.

Nancy's response was less than enthusiastic: "How do you know what I am believing? You have never even asked me."

John bolted back into the conversation. "I have just learned that Jesus is the only one who has a true view of who we are. If we focus on who Jesus says we are, we will find hope and strength. If we focus on who *we* think we are, we will find discouragement. I know it works!"

"John, I think that is great but . . ."

"Nancy, I have just taken a big step of growth in my life, and I have to tell you about it. I hope you will forgive me, but I have been struggling with pornography for years, and I have just seen the way out. I have believed the lie that sexual joy is found solely in exciting experiences, and I have let pornography take your place. I just discovered the answer is believing that Jesus loves me and has an answer for me in a living relationship with him. Nancy, you can find the same victory too!"

"John, I am glad you have found a way to grow. It's great to see.

But how can you tell me what I need without listening to me first? You just don't know."

This conversation ended with tension in the air. But an interesting thing happened. Nancy found she was feeling better about their marriage even though she didn't like the way John had tried to give her an easy solution for her own struggles. She had hope that she didn't really understand. As days passed she realized that a weight had been taken off her shoulders. Up to this time she had felt she was somehow responsible to get John to change. Now he was being changed by the grace of God!

Frustration with your spouse can become a way of life. As a wife, you may get impatient with your husband's inability to express his own emotions, followed by his all-too-convenient solutions to your emotional needs. You may become exasperated by your husband's bad habits and possible addictions. You can become discouraged when your dreams and goals are treated with contempt by the man of your dreams.

As a husband, you may get angry over the way your wife spends money. You may feel she is too emotional to think clearly, and so you leave her out of many decisions in your life. You may build up resentment because you think she is insensitive to your sexual needs.

A wife can find hope in the fact that God will address in her husband the areas that need growth. A husband can likewise find hope in the fact that God will address in his wife the areas that need growth. This is what Nancy discovered. She didn't like the way John jumped to conclusions about her life, but she felt hope that John would continue to grow. God had his attention, and if God could deal with John in the area of pornography, maybe he could also work with John to make him more sensitive and patient.

Of course, to verbalize your spiritual life you need to *have* a spiritual life. This life begins by understanding and acting on four very basic pieces of truth.

1. God trusted us with life. In his wisdom and kindness, God created us as living beings who have physical and spiritual life.

2. We broke the trust. Adam and Eve started the rebellion by deciding to do things their own way rather than follow God's clear instructions. We have followed their example by choosing to do things our own way rather than follow the principles clearly spelled out in the Bible. This decision to do things our own way is what the Bible calls sin.

3. God the Father has entrusted to Jesus the function of paying the penalty for our sin. Jesus died on the cross to pay the price we owe for our shortcomings. Jesus rose from the dead so he could give us his life. God has been pleased to accept all that Jesus has done as a sufficient substitute for what we could not do on our own.

4. If we trust Jesus to represent us before God, he will give us forgiveness and eternal life. We gain our spiritual life as a gift. We cannot earn it any more than we can earn our physical birth. We trust Jesus to give it to us. A simple way to express this trust is through prayer. The following is a suggested prayer:

Lord Jesus, I need you. I confess that I have done things my own way rather than trusting in your ways. I thank you that you died on the cross for my sins. From this day forward I will trust that your death and resurrection have secured eternal life for me. I will no longer trust my own efforts to be good enough to impress you. Please come into my life, forgive all that I've done wrong, and begin making me the kind of person you want me to be.

Your spiritual journey starts with a prayer of trust and is maintained by practicing "spiritual disciplines." The simplest of these are consistent Bible reading, daily prayer and talking with others about your spiritual growth. As you practice these disciplines, you can bring your spouse into the process by discussing a few questions with one another on a regular basis: "What has God taught you recently?" "What areas of your life is God working on that I can pray about for you?" "While we were at church today, what stood out to you?" "What are you praying about for our kids? for your friends?" You need to be careful not to interrogate one another with these questions as if your spouse is on trial, but you also need to be courageous in discussing these things with the one who shares the rest of your life.

Nancy doesn't agree with everything John does; sometimes she thinks his judgment is really off the wall! But she appreciates his unselfish motives. She says, "John is not a selfish man. It is a lot easier to trust a godly man even when we disagree."

Venture into Intimacy
The second skill in building trust is to *pursue intimacy with one another when answers are not obvious.* When the answer is obvious, by all means just do it! But situations that are not easily resolved are not reasons to reject each other. They are good times to seek to get to know one another better through good listening and discussion of how this situation is affecting each of you. Once you learn something new about your spouse through the situation, new possibilities generally arise because you trust one another enough to look at new options.

"Susie, we need more time together," Roger said with anxious longing in his heart. The last time they had this conversation Roger had been angry about his wife being gone at work while he was home with their preschool daughter.

"I know, Roger, but I don't see how we can do that right now. You yourself said we need to make more money, and my new job will get our bills paid."

"Yes, our bills will be paid, but we won't have a marriage if we don't see each other more," Roger shot back with an air of urgency in his voice.

"Well, if you would just stay up longer and wait for me to get home we could have more time together," Nancy answered abruptly. "You always want me to change to meet your needs. Why don't you change this time?"

"You know I need my sleep. Without enough sleep I just can't function at work, and we need my income. This would be simple to solve if we just put Kristen in day care and you worked during the day when I do," Roger said, defending his position.

"Maybe it would be simple for you, but what about Kristen and me? I don't want Kristen to be raised by other people! My mom put me in day care and I felt abandoned by her. In another year and a half she will be in kindergarten, and we won't even need to have this conversation."

"You want me to live like this for a year and a half?" Roger fired back.

"I don't want to make you miserable, Roger, but I can't agree to put Kristen into day care. We're the ones who need to raise her, not other people!" It was obvious to Roger that Nancy was not going to see things his way, so he just walked away in disgust to get lost in a project in his garage.

Roger and Nancy are locked in a situation for which they think there is no solution. Roger thinks Nancy could solve it by letting Kristen go to day care, but Nancy is not willing to do so, for reasons Roger does not understand. Nancy thinks Roger could solve this by sacrificing his sleep for a few months for the sake of her and their daughter. As a result, Roger and Nancy are starting to entertain thoughts that they cannot trust each other.

This is a situation in life that has no obvious answer. These situations are usually caused by the characteristics in your spouse that caused you to fall in love in the first place. Roger was attracted to Nancy because she was sensitive but firm in her decisions in life. She cared deeply for him and seemed willing to make whatever sacrifice was necessary to make his life more complete. He felt special around her because she was so attentive to what he needed. Now that her attentiveness is directed toward Kristen, he is feeling neglected. He is afraid that his needs will be sacrificed so that Kristen can be protected.

Nancy was attracted to Roger because he was level-headed and decisive. She felt a sense of stability and security when she was with him, because his approach to life was simple. Now that he wants to simplify their life together, she feels he is being insensitive to vital needs in their daughter's life and dismissing her concerns. In addition, Nancy is struggling with flashbacks to her past, which was characterized by neglect and abuse. She was hesitant to bring this into the conversation because she thought Roger would call it an excuse. If he could accept her struggle he might understand.

The real need here is intimacy. Roger needs to tap into the intense need Nancy has to protect Kristen's development. Nancy needs to understand that when Roger's life gets too complicated he becomes unresponsive to the emotional needs of those around him.

"Nancy," ventured Roger, "I want to try to understand why this is such a difficult issue to discuss. Can we talk about this without having to make a decision?"

"Well, will you really listen or will you just try to fix things?" replied Nancy with hesitation in her voice.

"I don't really understand why this is such a big issue to you, and I can see we are going to get nowhere if we don't understand each other better," said Roger, with a compassion that surprised Nancy.

Nancy still works at night and they are still taking turns watching Kristen, but they have hope again and they are discussing some new options. They are considering having Nancy work two part-time jobs instead of one full-time one, so that only half her hours are at night. They are also exploring the possibility of having Nancy develop a home-based business so she can be home more. They have even discussed moving to a place with a lower standard of living in hopes of living on one income. They still don't have their answer, but they have found a closeness with one another that allows them to work together in trust rather than work against each other in competition.

Value Your Mate

The third skill to developing trust is to *establish a track record of sacrificing for the good of your mate.* Your spouse is the most valuable person in your life. The more your spouse believes this, the more trust you will receive. It would be ideal if we treated our loved ones with as much care on ordinary days as we do during a crisis.

Our lives are filled with storms, but sometimes we are so used to them that we act as if they aren't even there. Life transitions, time demands, temptations and boredom are all fronts which can tear our lives apart if we aren't braced for the impact. If a physical storm endangered the life of your spouse, you would do whatever was necessary to offer protection. Watch out for the emotional storms which endanger the life of your marriage. Do whatever is necessary to protect your heart from forgetting the value of your spouse.

Lynn and Steve Dannheisser were an average couple living in an average neighborhood in Florida, but August 24, 1992, was anything but an average day. It was the day Hurricane Andrew ripped through Miami. Thinking a home out of the path of the storm surge would be safer, Lynn and Steve bundled up their children and traveled to Ira and Ruth's. Lynn laid out the sleeping bags in the largest closest she could find, and her family climbed in. She kissed her children good night and they dozed off.

The wind began to howl. The French doors rattled violently. Steve and Ira barricaded the doors with the heavy wooden kitchen table. The backyard fence tumbled away like a child's toy in the wind. For safety, everyone was moved into the windowless hallway and all the doors leading to the hallway were shut. Suddenly there was a huge crash from one of the bedrooms. Something had smashed in the window. The next moment, the bedroom ceiling collapsed. Then water began to flood into the hall.

Ruth ran into her bedroom to get something, and as she ran out that ceiling collapsed also. Lynn grabbed all the kids and retreated to the only closet left—in the only bedroom still intact. The walls of the house shook. The roof tiles made loud popping sounds as they flew off. Barely audible were the whimpering sounds of children crying. Lynn tried to comfort them, but her own heart raced with panic.

Ira yelled from the living room that the front doors were about to give way. Steve and Ira leaned against them with all their combined strength. Water was rising and soaking the carpet in their closet hideaway. Ruth and Lynn decided it was time to move the kids again. One by one, they fled down the hallway and into the family room. As the last one passed, the hallway ceiling crashed down, leaving a pile of gray sludge and debris where the group had been standing just moments before. The air was stale and hot and smelled of seawater.

Finally, about three and a half hours later, the wind began to die down. The group tumbled outside for a look at the now stark and desolate landscape. Exhausted, they slept on the only dry mattress in the house for an hour.

Lynn and Steve decided they needed to venture back to their own neighborhood. Steve held Lynn and said, "You need to prepare yourself. We may not have much of a house left." As the couple walked toward their neighborhood, Lynn silently chanted, *It's going to be okay. It's going to be okay.*

Then they spotted it. Part of the roof was missing. Their son's basketball pole had been launched through a window. Inside, the walls were plastered with dirt and leaves; there was water everywhere, cracks in the ceiling and garage; but for the most part, they had a house. Lynn recalls the emotion of the moment, "As Steve and I took it all in, we began to jump up and down like children. . . . For the moment, we felt we were blessed."[1]

Life's torrents will come your way. When the whirlwind hits your home, wrap your arms around each other and say, "I will protect you. You will protect me. We will protect the children. With God's help, we will get through this—*together.*"

*   *   *

Time Out of the Tornado

Find ways to say "I trust you." Write a note saying why you find it easy to trust him or her in some area of life. Or think of something your spouse has done that really bothered you. Say to your spouse, "You are more important than my right to be angry. I do love you!" Write down a verse that you think might encourage him or her. Or open up and share a special longing you have or a memory that is difficult for you. Be vulnerable!

If you are at a point where these suggestions seem impossible, pray for your spouse. Ask God to intercede—to reestablish trust within your marriage. Then trust that God is going to do it.

Notes

Chapter 1: How Did We Get in This Whirlwind?

[1]David Fisher, *The Scariest Place on Earth* (New York: Random House, 1994), p. 87.

[2]"Time Marches Inexorably On," *USA Today,* Mar. 1992, p. 7.

[3]Charles Swindoll, "Words of Promise," *Pursuit,* Fall 1995, p. 22.

[4]Fisher, *Scariest Place on Earth,* p. 175.

[5]Ibid., p. 182.

Chapter 5: Transitions

[1]Adapted from Marital Satisfaction Chart.

[2]Jim and Sally Conway, *Women in Mid-Life Crisis* (Wheaton, Ill.: Tyndale House, 1983), p. 112.

[3]Ibid., p. 129.

[4]Sally Conway and Jim Conway, *When a Mate Wants Out* (Grand Rapids, Mich.: Zondervan, 1992), p. 72.

[5]"Can't You Hear What I Am Thinking?" *Marriage Partnership,* Winter 1993, p. 35.

Chapter 6: Goal Setting

[1]Emilie Barnes, *The Creative Home Organizer* (Eugene, Ore.: Harvest House, 1988), p. 15.

[2]Patrick Morley, *The Man in the Mirror* (Brentwood, Tenn.: Wolgemuth & Hyatt, 1989), p. 84.

[3]Robert Barner, "The New Career Strategist," *Futurist,* Sept.-Oct. 1994, p. 10.

[4]Ibid., p. 14.

Chapter 8: Technology

[1]Connie Willis, "Jurassic Park and Al Jolson: Thinking About the Information Revolution," *Information Technology and Libraries*, Mar. 1994, p. 54.

[2]William Halal, "The Information Technology Revolution," *Futurist*, Jul.-Aug. 1992, p. 12.

[3]Leslie Crawford, "Visionaries Picture the Superhighway," *PC World*, Feb. 1994, p. 139.

[4]Ibid.

[5]Nicholas Negroponte, "What's in It for Me?" *Modern Maturity*, Feb.-Mar. 1994, p. 27.

[6]Joshua Macht, "Verbatim: How Has Technology Changed the Way You Do Your Job?" *Inc.*, technology issue, 1994, p. 36.

[7]Quoted in a Nov. 15, 1995, seminar by The Edge Group, P.O. Box 5005, Rancho Santa Fe, CA 92067.

Chapter 10: The Sequencing Options

[1]David Sharp, "Family vs. Career," *USA Weekend*, Dec. 2-4, 1994, p. 6.

[2]"News Anchor to Head *Inside Edition* Soon," *Times Advocate*, Oct. 22, 1994, p. A2.

[3]Bettina Lankard, "The Changing Work Force Trends and Issues," U.S. Dept. of Education report, Olsten Corp. Forum on Human Resources and Trends, 1992 (Columbus, Ohio: ERIC Clearinghouse), p. 14.

[4]"New Staffing Strategies for the 90s," U.S. Dept. of Education report, study commissioned by the Olsten Corp. Forum on Human Resource Issues and Trends, 1991, p. 5.

[5]Other options for facts and figures on various career trends are (1) ERIC Clearinghouse on Adult Career and Vocational Education, 1900 Kenny Rd., Columbus, OH 43210-1090; (2) Olsten Corporation, 175 Broad Hollow Rd., Melville, NY 11747.

[6]Monograph: *Balancing Work and Family* (Columbus: Center for Sex Equality/Ohio State University, 1994), p. 5.

[7]"New Staffing Strategies for the 90s," p. 9.

[8]Ibid., pp. 9-10.

Chapter 11: The Aggressive Options

[1]Susan Solomon Yem, "Heading Home," *Virtue*, Jan.-Feb. 1995, p. 43.

[2]Amy Dunkin, "Taking Care of Business Without Leaving the House," *Business Week*, Apr. 17, 1995, p. 106.

[3]Ibid., p. 43.

[4]Ibid., p. 106.

[5]Nancy Chambers, Lisa Kalis, Anne Nelson, Hagar Scher and Melissa Schorr, "25 Hottest Careers for Women," *Working Woman*, July 1995, pp. 32-33.

[6]Lindsey O'Connor, *Working at Home* (Eugene, Ore.: Harvest House, 1990), p. 16.

[7]Chambers et al., "25 Hottest Careers for Women," p. 33.

[8]Sandra Kerka, "Women and Entrepreneurship," *ERIC Digest,* no. 143, Ohio State University, Columbus, 1993, p. 3.

[9]Ibid., p. 2.

[10]Ibid.

[11]Eric Winslow and George Solomon, "Entrepreneurs Are More Than Nonconformists: They Are Mildly Sociopathic," *Journal of Creative Behavior,* vol. 21, no. 3, 1987, p. 203.

[12]Ronaleen Roha, "Call Your Own Shots," *Kiplinger's Personal Finance Magazine,* Jun. 1992, p. 46.

[13]Dunkin, "Taking Care of Business," p. 107.

[14]Fiona McQuarrie, "Telecommuting: Who Really Benefits?" *Business Horizons,* Nov.-Dec. 1994, p. 80.

[15]Conall Ryan, "Alone Again, Unnaturally," *Inc.,* Jan. 1994, p. 22.

Chapter 12: The Strenuous Options

[1]Charlene Marmer, "The Split-Shift Family," *Parents,* Mar. 1995, p. 102.

[2]Ricki Fulman, "You Work, He Works: But in Different Cities," *Cosmopolitan,* Nov. 1993, p. 243.

Chapter 13: The Unexpected Options

[1]"Good News for Mr. Moms," *Woman's Day,* Jul. 19, 1994, p. 29. For a sample of *At-Home Dad* newsletter, send SASE to Peter Baylies, *At-Home Dad,* 61 Brightwood Ave., North Andover, MA 01845.

Chapter 14: Protecting Your Relationship with Trust

[1]Lynn Dannheisser, "One Year Later: Diary of a Hurricane Survivor," *Redbook,* Aug. 1993, p. 110.